# Full Illumination
of the Path to Enlightenment

A Concise Commentary on Atiśa's
'Lamp of the Path to Enlightenment'

**Series** Ganesha Press

ABOUT GANESHA PRESS

Ganesha Press is the publishing house of Dechen, an international association of Sakya and Kagyu Buddhist centres and groups founded by Lama Jampa Thaye under the authority of Karma Thinley Rinpoche.

# Full Illumination of the Path to Enlightenment

A Concise Commentary on Atiśa's
'Lamp of the Path to Enlightenment'

JAMGON KONGTRUL LODRO THAYE

Translated by Adrian O'Sullivan

FULL ILLUMINATION OF THE PATH TO ENLIGHTENMENT
Copyright © 2024 Ganesha Press Limited

This edition by Rabsel Publications in partnership with Ganesha Press and Dechen Foundation Books.

GANESHA PRESS
121 Sommerville Road, St Andrews, Bristol, BS6 5BX, UK

All rights reserved. No part of this book may be reproduced, stored in or introduced in a retrieval system, or transmitted in any form or by any means (electronic, mechanical, photocopying, recording or otherwise) without prior written permission from the publisher or author, except for the inclusion of brief quotations in a review or for the private use of readers.

RABSEL PUBLICATIONS
16, rue de Babylone
76430 La Remuée, France
www.rabsel.com
contact@rabsel.com

© Rabsel Publications, La Remuée, France, 2024
ISBN 978-2-36017-063-0

## Contents

Foreword ........................................................................3
Introduction..................................................................5
Lamp of the Path to Enlightenment..............................21
Full Illumination of the Path to Enlightenment.............35
Notes.........................................................................129

# Foreword

I am delighted to welcome Adrian O'Sullivan's fine new translation of Jamgon Kongtrul Lodro Thaye's commentary on Atiśa's *Lamp of the Path to Enlightenment*. Atiśa's *Lamp of the Path to Enlightenment*, authored in 1043 during this celebrated master's time in Tibet, is one of the most influential texts in Buddhist history. Bringing together the major elements of doctrine and practice, both sūtra and tantra, represented in the lineages of 'Profound View', 'Vast Activity' and 'Blessings', it has served as the inspiration for many of the works subsequently produced in the *lamrim* ('Stages of the Path') genre by masters belonging to Kagyu, Sakya and Gelug traditions.

*Lama Jampa Thaye,*
*London, September 2023*

# Introduction

The present text is a translation of Atiśa's (979-1053) *The Lamp of the Path to Enlightenment,* together with its commentary, *Full Illumination of the Path to Enlightenment,* by Jamgon Kongtrul Lodro Thaye (1813-1899).

Atiśa, also known as Dīpaṃkara Śrījñāna, was born in 979 in Sahor in Bengal into a royal family of great wealth and power. The late tenth century was a time of flourishing for Buddhist monasticism and the tantric teachings, and it was in this environment that Atiśa as a young man studied under many masters of the sūtras and tantras. At the great monastery of Nālandā, Atiśa received teachings on bodhicitta, the altruistic pursuit of the benefit of others through the achievement of enlightenment. Atiśa subsequently renounced his royal inheritance to dedicate his life to the teaching and practice of Buddhadharma for the benefit of others. He adopted the conduct of a tantric yogin, and had many visionary experiences of tantric deities, signs of his wisdom and spiritual accomplishment.

It was through one such vision that Atiśa encountered Śākyamuni Buddha himself, who advised Atiśa to take full monastic ordination as the most suitable means to bring benefit to sentient beings. Thus at the age of twenty-nine, at Bodhgayā in central India, Atiśa received ordination into the ancient Mahāsāṃghika lineage of monastic vows. Eventually, Atiśa would meet over one hundred and fifty masters, receiving countless teachings on sūtra, tantra, and worldly fields of knowledge such as grammar, poetics and epistemology.

Around 1012, out of his dedication to the development of bodhicitta, Atiśa took a perilous sea voyage to the island of Sumatra in search of the master Dharmakīrti, who was renowned for his possession of especially powerful teachings on bodhicitta. Dharmakīrti would become the master for whom Atiśa would subsequently express the highest devotion, due to the preciousness and power of the bodhicitta teachings Atiśa received from him. Following this transformative training, Atiśa returned to India in 1025, eventually accepting a preeminent role at the great monastic university of Vikramaśila. Thus Atiśa's life continued on the trajectory of a learned and accomplished master of the Buddhadharma in India.

This trajectory was to change however when, around 1033-34, several delegations of Tibetan monks began to appear at Vikramaśīla. They were intent on inviting Atiśa to visit Western Tibet where, under patronage of the Tibetan lords, Lha Lama Yeshe O and Lha Lama Changchub-O, a great revival of study and practice of Buddhadharma was underway. Though uncertain about the viability or benefit of such an expedition, in visionary encounters, the goddess Tārā revealed to Atiśa that, although the trip would shorten his life, it would nevertheless bring great benefit to others. Disregarding self-interest and intent upon the benefit of others, Atiśa determined to undertake the journey. This was much to the delight of the Tibetan delegates, such as Ngaktso Lotsawa (1011-1064), who had undertaken great hardships to reach India and who had come to have great devotion to the noble master.

Atiśa, now over sixty years old, together with his delegation, eventually arrived in Ngari in Western Tibet in 1042, received with great joy and fanfare by the Tibetans, led by the lord Lha Lama Changchub-O. There, the warmth, gentleness and wisdom of Atiśa began to make an impression upon the Tibetans which communicates itself to us even today, through the recorded stories of his biographies. The Tibetans could see for themselves how Atiśa was the authentic embodiment the teachings of the Buddha, not least in his meticulous attention to the preservation of the vows of the three vehicles—Hīnayāna, Mahāyāna and Vajrayāna—to the extent that, if he found himself making the slightest transgression of vows even in his thoughts, Atiśa would immediately confess and seek to purify the misdeed. Atiśa never neglected simple and modest practices of goodness and kindness, and never took on airs or showed any vanity, yet his learning, authority and mastery were evident to all. Most importantly for the posterity of the Buddhadharma, Atiśa set about resolving confusions the Tibetans had about how to practice dharma and about the relations between the teachings of the three vehicles.

It was during his time in Ngari that Atiśa composed the text translated in this work, *The Lamp of the Path to Enlightenment,* as requested by Lha Lama Changchub-O. This wonderful text, which came to be respected and studied in all the various traditions of Buddhadharma that would later spread throughout Tibet, distinguishes three types of person: inferior, intermediate and superior. The inferior person seeks the means for their own happiness in this life and the next. The intermediate person seeks to attain liberation from saṃsāra for their own individual benefit. The superior person develops bodhicitta, seeking enlightenment for the benefit of all sentient beings. *The Lamp of the Path to Enlightenment* defines the three paths and sets out in full the stages of the path of the superior person, of which the other two paths are, in the final analysis, preliminary parts. Thus we are guided towards the Mahāyāna practice of Taking Refuge in the Three Jewels, and on to the development of the two aspects of bodhicitta—aspiration and application—which culminate in the development of wisdom and skilful means, and the final result of this—the enlightenment of a Buddha. Finally, Atiśa makes clear that the role of Vajrayāna on the path is to provide the means to accomplish its results swiftly and with ease. In composing the text, Atiśa brought three lineages together into a single stream: the 'Lineage of the Vast Activity' of teachings transmitted from Maitreya, Asaṅga and Vasubandhu; the 'Lineage of Profound View' transmitted from Mañjuśrī, Nāgārjuna and Candrakīrti; and the 'Lineage of Blessings', the source of the tantric teachings transmitted from Vajrayāna masters such as Nāropā.

*The Lamp of the Path to Enlightenment* arranges, contextualises and resolves doubts concerning countless teachings of the sūtras and tantras, many of which the Tibetans had previously thought to be irreconcilable. In doing so, it gave the Tibetans the confidence, clarity and understanding that would allow the Buddhadharma to flourish and propagate for centuries to come, even to the recent spreading of the teachings from Tibet to the rest of the world. *The Lamp of the Path to Enlightenment* and the model of the Three Persons would subsequently inspire other classic works of Tibetan dharma literature, a genre which came to be called in Tibetan '*lamrim*', meaning 'Stages of the Path'.

After three years in Western Tibet, Atiśa was expected to return to India. However, at this time, a Tibetan lay master called Dromton Gyalwa'i Jungne (1005-1064) arrived to invite Atiśa to give teachings in central Tibet. This event was in fact the fulfilment of a prophesy given to Atiśa by Tārā—that the master's most important disciple in Tibet would be a layman. Recognising the fulfilment of this prophesy had come, Atiśa blessed Dromton, and in due course he undertook the journey to central Tibet. There, at the burgeoning dharma centres and monasteries, Atiśa turned the wheel of dharma countless times. Traditionally, it is said that the teachings given by Atiśa fall into three categories: the *gzhung* or textual tradition, which comprise the great works of Indian masters such as Nāgārjuna, Asaṅga, Candrakīrti and Śāntideva; the *gdams ngag* or oral instructions tradition, which includes the bodhicitta teachings of Dharmakīrti and other masters; and thirdly the *man ngag*, or esoteric instructions tradition, which comprise the initiations and practices of the tantras.

Atiśa travelled widely around central and southern Tibet, giving the teachings of the three categories. Together with his close Tibetan disciples, he translated many Indian texts into Tibetan, including *The Lamp of the Path to Enlightenment* and his other compositions. After about seven years of such activity, Atiśa retired to Nyethang in the southern Kyichu valley, south of Lhasa, where he nightly experienced visions of Buddhas, bodhisattvas and deities. He predicted to his disciples that he would soon take rebirth in the Tuṣita heaven in the presence of the bodhisattva Maitreya. Fulfilling this prediction, Atiśa passed away in 1054 among many miraculous signs. His remains were enshrined by Dromton, and many precious articles and substances, some of ancient Indian origin, were bequeathed to his disciples. His disciples would go on to found monasteries and dharma communities based on Atiśa's teachings, of which the most famous is the Kadampa school, founded by Dromton. As my teacher, Lama Jampa Thaye said in remembering Atiśa's kindness, 'All of us look back to Atiśa as an extraordinary figure, whose blessings are still present in our practice.'

## Jamgon Kongtrul Lodro Thaye

The author of the present commentary to the *Lamp of the Path to Enlightenment* was the master known as Jamgon Kongtrul Lodro Thaye, an incarnation of Mañjuśrī, the bodhisattva of wisdom. Jamgon Kongtrul was born in 1813 in the kingdom of Derge in Eastern Tibet to a Bonpo family. At the age of sixteen, he was taken under the wing of a local chieftain and impressed those whom he met with his brilliance and ability. This led him in due course to the Nyingma monastery of Zhechen where he embarked upon a formal and rigorous education. At Zhechen, the young Jamgon Kongtrul received many dharma teachings, including blessings and initiations of the Vajrayāna. He took ordination in the 'lower' (Tib. *smad lugs*) lineage of monastic vows preserved in the Nyingma tradition, a lineage which dates back to Bodhisattva Śāntarakṣita's arrival in Tibet in the eighth century.

In 1833, at the age of twenty, Jamgon Kongtrul went to the major Karma Kagyu monastery of Palpung, established in 1727 by the powerful master, Tai Situ Chokyi Jungne (1700-1774). There Jamgon Kongtrul met the ninth Tai Situ, Pema Nyingje Wangpo (1775-1853), who would become one of his main teachers. Jamgon Kongtrul also took re-ordination there, this time in the "upper" (Tib. stod lugs) lineage of vows stemming from the thirteenth century Kashmiri master, Śākyaśrī Bhadra. This event impressed upon Jamgon Kongtrul the existence of divisions between institutions and traditions caused by their sectarian affiliations; by contrast, his life would go on to exemplify a nonsectarian attitude that would be productive of a remarkable legacy, as we shall see. Also while at Palpung, he was recognised by the Tai Situ as an incarnation of a recently deceased tulku from Bamteng in Kongpo. While this recognition would ensure that Jamgon Kongtrul be allowed to remain at Palpung, he himself saw it as a practical expediency rather than a spiritual reality. Later, as he rose to prominence, Jamgon Kongtrul would be recognised by Tai Situ and other leading masters of the time as an incarnation of great such beings of India and Tibet as the Buddha's attendant and cousin, Ānanda; the 8th century Tibetan translator and Dzogchen master Bairotsana; the 11th century Tibetan adept and scholar, Khyungpo Naljor, and many others. Nevertheless, the name of the Kongpo tulku ('Kongtrul') would stick, though it was made more honorific by the prefixing of the Tibetan name of Mañjuśrī ('Jamgon'), the bodhisattva who embodies wisdom and learning.

For the next few years, Kongtrul Rinpoche would receive countless teachings of sūtra and tantra from many masters at Palpung and other places, and indeed over the course of his life he would never tire in his pursuit of teachings. He showed extraordinary diligence in study and memorisation, and practiced a variety of strict meditation retreats, during which he had repeated visions and indications of spiritual accomplishment. He met the Fourteenth Karmapa (1798-1868) and received from him the bodhisattva vow and the bodhisattva name 'Lodro Thaye', meaning 'limitless intelligence'. In addition to his studies and meditation practices, Kongtrul Rinpoche took up the responsibilities of teacher, giving teachings and conducting ceremonies and religious service for the local people and their rulers, in particular at the royal court of Derge.

Beginning around the late 1840's, with the guidance and encouragement of the omniscient master Jamyang Khyentse Wangpo (1820-1892), Kongtrul Rinpoche began work on the first of what would eventually become five great non-sectarian textual collections, the so-called *Five Treasuries*. Khyentse Wangpo himself would, by the mid-1850s, produce the vast collection of initiation texts and practice rituals known as *The Collection of All Sadhanas,* which has today become one of the most widely utilised resources for the preservation and transmission of the deity practices of the 'new tantra' traditions. The *Five Treasuries* and *The Collection of All Sadhanas* preserve a vast array of dharma teachings and facilitate their transmission, including many that had come close to extinction. These great collections would later be expanded, transmitted and republished by the masters who were heirs to this tradition, such as the fifteenth

Karmapa, Khakyab Dorje (1870-1921) and Jamgon Loter Wangpo (1847-1914), ensuring their continued propagation. Indeed the latter master, Loter Wangpo, completed another vast collection begun but not completed by Khyentse Rinpoche, the *Collection of All Tantras,* comprising the empowerments, manuals and rituals for 132 maṇḍalas of the four sets of tantra. It is hard to imagine that, without such works, anything but a fraction of the Buddhdharma in Tibet would have survived the political upheavals of the twentieth century.

For Kongtrul Rinpoche, the first of the *Five Treasuries* he embarked upon was the *Treasury of the Kagyu School,* preserving and reinvigorating the major empowerments and associated rituals of that tradition. Then in the 1860s, he completed the encyclopaedic *Treasury of the Knowledge of Omniscience.* Then the *Treasury of Spiritual Advice* gathered many profound meditation instructions from eight major practice lineages of Tibet, following a structure and contents advised by Khyentse Rinpoche. The largest of the *Five Treasuries,* the *Treasury of Precious Termas,* collects revelatory 'treasure' teachings from over one hundred *tertons* or treasure revealers of the Nyingma tradition, a project which took Kongtrul over thirty years to complete. Finally the *Treasury Great and Vast,* again compiled in accord with Khyentse Rinpoche's guidance, contains many of Kongtrul Rinpoche's own commentaries, explanations and practice manuals, including works relating to his own revelatory termas. These *Five Treasuries,* even before they were expanded by later masters, comprised over ninety volumes, each volume comprising about six hundred pages.

Of the hundreds of texts that make up these great collections, many are compositions by earlier masters of India and Tibet which Kongtrul and Khyentse were able to include without alteration. However, in their dedication to preserving the teachings in a way that was accessible to students, Kongtrul and Khyentse had often to restore works relating to transmission lineages that had declined or which seemed incomplete, by writing texts anew, replacing missing parts, adding essential clarifying instructions, and updating lineage records and histories. They did so in ways that always remained faithful and deeply respectful to the original sources and lineages, whether that lineage was widespread and famous, or rare and arcane, in a spirit that would come to be called *rime* (Tib. *ris med*), i.e. 'boundaryless'.

Concerning the root verses and commentary of Atiśa's *Lamp of the Path to Enlightenment*, the texts translated in this book, these are preserved in the *Treasury of Spiritual Advice*. Two of the fourteen volumes in that collection are dedicated to the works of the Kadampa tradition, founded by Atiśa's main Tibetan disciple, Dromton. The *Lamp of the Path to Enlightenment* is the first text presented in those two volumes. The commentary, which was produced by Kongtrul Rinpoche himself in fulfilment of a direct instruction from Khyentse Rinpoche, comes as the fourth text in the same volume.

Kongtrul Rinpoche's commentary is based closely upon earlier authoritative works. One key source is a commentary on Atiśa's text by Panchen Lozang Chokyi Gyaltsen (1570-1662), entitled *A Feast of Exquisite Joy, Explaining the Lamp of the Path to Enlightenment* (*byang chub lam gyi sgron ma'i rnam bshad phul byung shad pa'i dga' ston*). Panchen Lozang Chokyi Gyaltsen in turn based his commentary on earlier authoritative works. As he says in his colophon, he relied on the auto-commentary (i.e. of Atīśa), the commentary of Naktso Lotsawa, the recorded sayings of Dromton himself and the latter's disciple Potowa (1027-1105), the *Blue Compendium* of Geshe Dolpa (1059-1131), the graduated path instructions of Potowa's student Sharawa (1070-1141), and other extant Kadam teachings. In short, the commentary is informed not only by Atīśa himself but also many of the early masters of the Kadampa tradition, each of whom were exemplary practitioners and communicators of Atiśa's heart advice. The faithful use of such sources is an essential feature of an authentic commentarial tradition, for it is only what accords with the teachings of the Omniscient One, the Buddha, that has the power to liberate. As the bodhisattva Maitreya famously says in the *Uttaratantraśāstra*,

> In this world, there is no one wiser than the Victor,
> No other one anywhere who is omniscient and properly knows supreme true reality in its entirety.

> Therefore, one should not deviate from the
> sūtras taught to be definitive by the Seer
> himself.
> Otherwise, this will harm the genuine
> dharma through destroying the guidance of
> the Sage.

This injunction is also exemplified by Atiśa who, at the end of *The Lamp of the Path to Enlightenment,* confirms the sources of his teaching:

> I, the Sthavira Dīpaṃkaraśrī,
> Have given this brief explanation of the path
> to enlightenment,
> As I have seen it explained in teachings such
> as the sūtras.

In addition to his reliance on the commentary of Panchen Lozang Chokyi Gyaltsen, there are two long passages in Kongtrul Rinpoche's commentary based closely on excerpts from *The Graduated Path to Enlightenment, the Practices of the Three Persons (skyes bu gsum gyi nyams su blang ba'i byang chub lam rim pa),* sometimes called the 'Middle Length Lamrim', by the Gelugpa patriarch Tsongkhapa Lozang Drakpa (1357-1419). The first passage is an overview of the stages of the path that elaborates on each of the Three Persons. The second passage sets out in detail the Madhyamaka or 'Middle Way' view following its prāsaṅgika or 'consequentialist' understanding, which Atiśa upheld. Kongtrul Rinpoche elsewhere holds as supreme the school of Madhyamaka known as 'Zhentong' or 'Empty of Other', which he sets out in works such as the *Treasury of the Knowledge of Omniscience*. In the present text, he demonstrates the *rime* spirit in seeking to remain true to Atiśa's prāsaṅgika position. Kongtrul does so by presenting it according to the teachings of Tsongkhapa and Panchen Lozang Chokyi Gyaltsen, whom he regards as flawless sources of the Kadampa teachings.

Through the *Five Treasuries* and other remarkable accomplishments in a variety of fields, Kongtrul Rinpoche's fame and reputation grew. His activities and projects in the later decades of his life seem boundless: solitary meditation retreats and extensive group monastic rituals; the transmission of countless teachings, including training many important masters of the subsequent generation; the ritual construction and consecration of stupas, statues, paintings and holy sites; the building, blessing, preparation and oversight of meditation and retreat centres; the establishment and ongoing facilitation of a three-year retreat programme; the printing of vast textual collections—not only each of the *Five Treasuries* but other holy collections such as the *Kangyur*, *Tengyur*, the collected Nyingma Tantras and so on. In short, Kongtrul Rinpoche worked tirelessly in service of the teachings and for the benefit of all. He did so despite some recurrent health problems, including a painful eye condition that also obscured his sight, for which at least he was eventually able to find some respite through the blessings of great treasure revealer, Chokgyur Dechen Lingpa (1829-1870), a master with whom both Kongtrul and Khyentse collaborated over many years.

INTRODUCTION

Kongtrul Rinpoche became the teacher of some of the greatest lamas of the next generation, including Jamgon Loter Wangpo (1847-1914), the Fifteenth Karmapa Khakyab Dorje (1870-1921), the Nyingma master and outstanding scholar, Jamgon Ju Mipham Gyatso (1846-1912), the venerable Khenchen Tashi Özer (1836-1910), and others too numerous to mention. Such masters received, mastered, and passed on the *Five Treasuries*, safeguarding the precious legacy for succeeding generations. Kongtrul Rinpoche passed away among his close students and attendants in 1899, at the age of 87, at the hermitage he had established decades before in the quiet recesses above Palpung, at a holy site called Tsadra Rinchen Drak.

There is no end to what could be said in praise of Atiśa, Jamgon Kongtrul and Jamyang Khyentse, and the great fortune of those who are able to receive even a tiny part of their legacy. One should consult their extensive biographical works for fuller accounts. Nevertheless, I hope that the foregoing will suffice as an introduction to the present translation. My sincere thanks and gratitude are due to all who have helped in the preparation and publication of this work.

Adrian O'Sullivan,
California, 2023

# Lamp of the Path to Enlightenment

*In the language of India: Bodhipathapradīpa. In Tibetan: byang chub lam gyi sgron ma [Lamp of the Path to Enlightenment].*

I bow down to the bodhisattva Mañjuśrī Kumārabhūta.

1
To all the Conquerors of the three times, their dharma,
And the saṅgha, I pay homage with great devotion.
At the urging of my good disciple Changchub-O,
I will shine a lamp of the path to enlightenment.

2
Lesser, intermediate and supreme:
Thus the Three Persons are to be known.
I shall write to clarify the distinctions
Between each of their natures.

3
Someone using methods by which
They pursue, for their own good,
Mere saṃsāric happiness,
Should be known as inferior.

4
Someone who turns away from conditioned happiness
And desists from nonvirtuous actions,
Seeking only their own individual peace,
Should be called an intermediate person.

5
Someone who, by their own suffering,
Truly wishes to completely end
All the sufferings of others
Is a superior person.

6
For those excellent beings
Who want supreme enlightenment,
I will now explain the authentic means
Which has been taught by the lamas.

7
Before an image of the perfect Buddha,
A stupa, and the holy dharma,
Make offerings with whatever you have—
Flowers, incense, materials etc.

8
With the seven point offering taught in
*Samanthabhadra's Prayer for Good Conduct*,

Until one's destination, the heart of enlightenment, is reached,
With the pure intention never to stop,

9
Have strong faith in the Three Jewels
And, placing one knee on the ground,
With one's palms together,
Begin by going for refuge three times.

10
Then, a loving intention towards
All sentient beings is the preliminary
To looking upon all beings, without exception,
Suffering throughout the three lower realms,
Birth, death, transmigration etc.

11
And wishing to set them free
From the sufferings that torment them,
From suffering, suffering, and its cause.
One should generate bodhicitta,
Which is an irreversible commitment.

12
That is the pure mind of aspiration.
The qualities of developing it
Have been well explained by Maitreya
In the *Gaṇḍavyūha Sūtra*.

13
One should read the sūtras or hear them from the lama,
For truly to understand the limitless qualities of the mind of perfect enlightenment

Will cause its stabilisation.
Again and again develop the intention in this way.

14
In the *Sūtra of Vīradatta's Questions*
Its merit is explained fully.
There, in just three of its verses,
It is summarised, which I will now quote.

15
"What merit there is in bodhicitta,
If it could have form,
Would fill the realms of space,
And overflow even from this."

16
"However many grains of sand there may be in
The Ganges, as many Buddha fields
Could be completely filled with gems
And offered by someone to the lords of the world,"

17
"But, if someone folds their hands
With devotion for enlightenment,
Their veneration is superior,
For there is no limit to that."

18
Having developed true aspiration bodhicitta,
One should always increase it with all kinds of exertion.
In order to remember this as well in other lives,
Maintain assiduously the trainings just as they are explained.

### 19

Unless one holds the vow of application bodhicitta,
Aspiration will not develop to perfection.
Those wishing to increase the vow of perfect
  enlightenment
Should definitely make effort to take this vow.

### 20

Apart from always holding
The seven kinds of prātimokṣa,
The good fortune of this bodhisattva vow
Is not to be found anywhere.

### 21

Among the seven kinds of prātimokṣa
Explained by the Tathāgata,
The glorious Brahmā conduct is supreme.
The vows of the bhikṣu are to be known thus.

### 22

One should know the excellent lama
To be learned in the ritual of the vow,
To be someone who keeps the vow,
And to consent to bestow the vow with compassion.

### 23

Using the ritual taught in the chapter
On moral discipline in the *Bodhisattvabhūmi*,
Take the vow from the excellent lama
Who possesses the requisite characteristics.

24
For one who has tried but been unable
To find such a qualified lama,
I shall properly explain another ritual
To take the vow.

25
In a past age, Mañjuśrī,
When he was Ambarāja,
Generated bodhicitta in the way
That is taught in the sūtra of
*The Ornament of Mañjuśrī's Buddha Realm*,
As I shall now relate here in full.

26
"In the presence of the Protectors,
I generate perfect bodhicitta.
Inviting all beings as my guests,
I will liberate them from saṃsāra."

27
"From now until I have attained
Perfect enlightenment, I will cease
Intentions of harm, aggression,
Greed and envy."

28
"I will practise pure conduct
And abandon nonvirtue and desire.
Taking joy in the vow of conduct,
I will train following the Buddhas."

29
"Taking no pleasure in swiftly
Attaining enlightenment for myself,
I will remain until the end
For even a single being."

30
"I will utterly purify
Inconceivable fields without limit.
For those who remember my name,
I will remain for them throughout the ten directions."

31
"I will purify entirely
Actions of body and speech.
I will purify the activity of mind too,
And I will cease nonvirtuous actions."

32
If one keeps the vow of application bodhicitta,
It is the cause of complete purification of body, speech, and mind.
If the moral conduct of the three trainings is properly practised,
Devotion to the moral conduct of the three trainings will grow greater.

33
Therefore, intent upon pure and perfect enlightenment,
Bodhisattvas will keep the vow of vows pure.
They will endeavour in perfect enlightenment
And completely fulfill the accumulations.

## 34
The cause of completely perfecting the accumulations,
The natures of which are merit and wisdom,
Is held by all the Buddhas
To be the development of the higher knowledges.

## 35
Just as a bird with unfledged wings
Cannot fly in the sky,
So, without the power of the higher knowledges,
One cannot benefit beings.

## 36
Whatever merit may be obtained in a single day
By someone endowed with the higher knowledges,
Will not be obtained in a hundred lifetimes
By someone who lacks them.

## 37
Those who want to complete swiftly
The accumulations of perfect enlightenment
Will accomplish the higher knowledges
Not through laziness but through effort.

## 38
Since without achieving calm abiding
The higher knowledges will not arise,
One should apply oneself again and again
In trying to accomplish calm abiding.

## 39
While the conditions of calm abiding are weak,
Even to meditate with strong diligence

For thousands of years
Will not accomplish samādhi.

40
Therefore, maintain well the conditions
Taught in the *Tract on the Accumulation of Samādhi*.
Place the mind in virtue
On any suitable object of attention.

41
When the yogin attains calm abiding,
The higher knowledges are attained also.
Yet without the yoga of the perfection of wisdom,
The obscurations will not be exhausted.

42
Therefore, in order to abandon completely
The obscurations of defilements and cognition,
Cultivate the perfection of wisdom
Always in conjunction with skilful means.

43
Wisdom without skilful means
And skilful means without wisdom
Were said to be prisons.
Do not therefore abandon either of them.

44
To eliminate doubts concerning
What 'wisdom' and 'skilful means' are,
I will now clarify the correct distinction
Between skilful means and wisdom.

## 45
Apart from the perfection of wisdom,
All virtuous dharmas,
Such as the perfection of giving,
Were taught by the Conquerors to be skilful means.

## 46
Whoever cultivates wisdom
Through the power of cultivating skilful means
Will soon attain enlightenment
But, by cultivating non-self alone, will not.

## 47
The skandhas, dhātus, and āyatanās
Are to be understood as being without arising.
This recognition of the emptiness of intrinsic nature
Is the definition of 'wisdom'.

## 48
Arising from existence is not logical,
Nor is arising from nonexistence, like a skyflower.
Consequently both are errors.
Therefore there is no arising from both, either.

## 49
Objects do not arise from self,
Nor from other, nor from both,
Nor without cause, because of which,
They have no intrinsic nature.

## 50
Or, if all dharmas
Are analysed for singularity and multiplicity,

Since no essence is seen,
It is certain they have no intrinsic nature.

51

The arguments of the *Seventy Verses on Emptiness,
The Root Verses on the Middle Way* and so forth,
Show the proofs for the emptiness
Of the intrinsic nature of things.

52

Because this text would become too long,
I will not elaborate on them here,
But I have fully explained just the established tenets
For the purpose of meditation.

53

Therefore, whoever meditates upon non-self
Without seeing an intrinsic nature
Of any dharma whatsoever
Is meditating upon wisdom.

54

Just as one with wisdom does not see
Any intrinsic nature in all dharmas,
So wisdom itself is subject to analysis.
One should meditate without any concepts.

55

This world comes from conceptual discrimination.
Its very core is conceptual discrimination.
Therefore, abandon such discrimination entirely.
That is the supreme nirvāṇa.

## 56
Thus the Bhagavān said,
'Conceptual discrimination is the great ignorance.
It plunges one into the ocean of saṃsāra.
Resting in non-discriminating samādhi,
Sky-like non-discrimination will be revealed.'

## 57
In the *Dhāraṇī of Entering into Non-discrimination Sūtra* it likewise says,
'Should sons of the Conquerors meditate upon
This sacred teaching of non-discrimination,
They will escape the struggles of discrimination,
And gradually achieve non-discrimination.'

## 58
With scriptures and reasoning,
Having made certain that all dharmas
Are nonarising, without intrinsic nature,
Meditate without discrimination.

## 59
Thus if one meditates upon suchness
And attains the successive stages of heat etc.,
Then one will attain the Joyful bhūmi and the rest,
And the enlightenment of a Buddha will not be far off.

## 60
With activities such as pacifying and increasing,
And also with powers such as the eight great attainments,
Like the excellent vase attainment,

Which are accomplished through the power of mantra,

61
If one wishes to fulfil completely with ease
The accumulations of enlightenment,
And if one wishes for the conduct of the secret mantras
Taught in Kriyā, Caryā etc. tantras,

62
Then, for the ācārya empowerment,
One should please the holy lama with all one has,
Such as with veneration and with gifts, such as jewels,
And by accomplishing his instructions.

63
The one who pleases the lama
Will perfectly receive the ācārya empowerment.
All of one's nonvirtues will be utterly purified
And one will become worthy of accomplishing siddhis.

64
Because the great *Paramādibuddha* tantra
Expressly forbids it,
Those observing pure conduct
Should not receive the secret and wisdom empowerments.

65
Should these empowerments be received
By those keeping the discipline of pure conduct,
Because its conduct has been forbidden,
Their vows of discipline would be broken.

## 66
This would be a defeat
Of the discipline they were holding and a downfall,
And since they would be sure to fall into the lower realms,
They could not attain siddhis.

## 67
Hearing and explaining all the tantras,
Performing fire pūjās, offerings, and so forth,
Are not faults for those who have received
The ācārya empowerment and know thusness.

## 68
Upon the supplication of Changchub-O,
I, the Sthavira Dīpaṃkaraśrī,
Have given this brief explanation of the path to enlightenment,
As I have seen it explained in teachings such as the sūtras.

*The Lamp of the Path to Enlightenment*, composed by the great ācārya Dīpaṃkara Śrījñāna is completed. It was translated and checked by the great master of India himself and the great translator and editor, Gewa'i Lodro.

# Full Illumination of the Path to Enlightenment

## A Concise Commentary on Atiśa's 'Lamp of the Path to Enlightenment'

I bow down with great respect before the feet of the Lord of the Śākyas.

> Displaying the flowers of the major marks, bearing one hundred merits, and the beautiful pollen bed of the minor signs,
> Sounding the melodious drum of the sixty qualities and revealing the path to the three kinds of trainees,
> The sky mirror of your primordial wisdom reflecting the reality of phenomena with clarity and distinctness,
> Supreme teacher, your kindness is unequalled.
> Please keep us in your heart and care for us with compassion.

Having generated supreme bodhicitta, one
   enters the path and dwells on the bhūmis.
This precious jewel of mind, which
   transforms whoever generates it,
Was revealed by you, possessing the three
   virtues, with excellent speech, upon a
   mandala of the sun and moon,
Where I pray you will always liberate the
   lotus flowers of faithful and devoted minds
   from rebirth.

In your limitless manifestations, you
   appeared in the Land of Snows,
As a son of the Conqueror, showing us the
   flawless liberation path,
A noble lord, whose victory banner is famed
   throughout the three realms,
I pay homage to the Lord Atiśa.

The holders of your lineage are the
   Kadampas, holding Buddha's words and
   oral instructions.
The pearl beads of the Teacher's ancient and
   new traditions,
Are threaded together with the golden cord
   of their life examples.
With devoted faith, I uphold them as my
   crown ornament.

Just to hear their words is conducive to
   liberation from conditioned existence,
But to practise them will accomplish the
   final goal.

> This authentic text is like a flawless lapis
> lazuli.
> It has been the foundation stone of the
> wealth of the Tibetan people.
>
> This system is as famous as the sun and
> moon
> And has already been thoroughly elucidated
> by many holy ones.
> Yet, may this simple commentary, which fills
> a small pot of understanding
> For someone like me, increase, if only a
> little, the nectar of this teaching.

*The Lamp of the Path to Enlightenment* contains the key points of all the teachings of the Conqueror, and is the pathway of the two charioteers—Nāgārjuna and Asaṅga, and the dharma tradition of the supreme ones travelling to the stage of omniscience, condensing everything into the stages of practice of the Three Persons, without omitting anything. The explanation of this has two parts:

1. The branches of the explanandum
2. The meaning of the main instructions

## 1. The branches of the explanandum

The scholars of Vikramaśīla asserted the importance of giving a preliminary account of three key points, which I will now briefly present:

1. The greatness of the author, in order to show the authenticity of the source of the teaching
2. The greatness of the teaching itself, in order to generate respect for the instructions
3. How a teaching with these two greatnesses should be heard and explained

## 1. The greatness of the author of the text

A bodhisattva of the Good Kalpa intentionally took rebirth within a great royal lineage in the land of Zahor. Having gained complete mastery over the qualities of scriptural knowledge of almost the entirety of the Three Baskets, and having gained complete mastery over the qualities of realisation through correct practice, in the Palace of Great Enlightenment at the Vajra Seat, three times he overcame the negative speech of the tīrthikas. With such deeds in both India and Tibet, he greatly spread the teachings of the Buddha. In particular, once he had come to Tibet, he turned limitless wheels of very profound and vast dharma. He wrote treatises such as the present *Lamp of the Path to Enlightenment* so that practices of the Conqueror's teachings which were in decline could be restored, and those which had been only slightly introduced would be elucidated. Thus everywhere he guided beings, whether directly or indirectly, on the inerrant paths of temporal happiness and definitive goodness. He is known as the great paṇḍita, the Noble Master, the glorious Atiśa. Naktso Lotsāwa[1] says in his *Eighty Verses of Praise*,

> Before the Noble Master's arrival in Tibet,
> All were as blind men.
> Once you, the spreader of knowledge, had arrived
> In Tibet, the sun of wisdom dawned.

## 2. The greatness of the teaching

The distilled essence of all the teachings of the Sage, the only lamp of the terrestrial, celestial and subterranean planes, the pathway of the two great charioteers, the pith instructions in which three rivers of transmission[2] merge, the great path of temporal happiness and definitive goodness, the key to unlock all the sūtras and their commentaries, the pathway trodden by all learned and accomplished masters of India and Tibet, is the treatise which sets out what is to be practised by the three kinds of person, without omitting anything: the *Lamp of the Path to Enlightenment*. Since it condenses the key points of both sūtra and mantra, its subject matter is fully comprehensive. Since it emphasises the training of sentient beings in graduated stages, it is easy to put into practice. Since it is adorned with the oral instructions of Atiśa's two teachers who were learned in the traditions of the two great charioteers,[3] it is superior to other traditions.

## 3. How a teaching with these two greatnesses should be heard and explained

How to hear the teaching, how to explain it, and practices common to both of these, are explained in detail in the detailed instruction manuals on the graduated path to enlightenment, so one can learn them from there.

## 2. The meaning of the main instructions

1. Title
2. Translator's homage
3. The text itself
4. Colophon

## 1. Title

**In the language of India: *Bodhipathapradīpa*. In Tibetan: byang chub lam gyi sgron ma [Lamp of the Path to Enlightenment].**

**In** Sanskrit, one of **the** four great **languages of** ancient **India**, the land of āryas, the title of this text is ***Bodhipathapradīpa*,** which is translated **into Tibetan** as ***byang chub lam gyi sgron ma****. Bodhi* is *byang chub* [enlightenment], *patha* is *lam* [path] and *pradīpa* is *sgron ma* [lamp]. The primordial wisdom of the Buddhas, who embody the perfection of abandonment and realisation, is the complete purification [*byang*] of the two obscurations, together with their imprints, and the complete mastery [*chub pa*] of all dharmas, as they seem and as they are: hence *byang chub* [enlightenment]. The obstacles to the path leading there are lack of understanding, misunderstandings and doubts. Since this śāstra completely dispels such darkness and illuminates the nature of the ten bhūmis and five paths, it is called a 'lamp'.

The Indian title of the text is stated at the beginning of the translation of the śāstra in order to demonstrate the authenticity of the source of the teaching, to generate gratitude and appreciation for the translators, scholars, the king and his ministers, to allow the reader to establish a connection with the Sanskrit language, and so forth.

## 2. Translator's homage

**I bow down to the bodhisattva Mañjuśrī Kumārabhūta.**

This homage has been inserted by the translator in order to indicate that, while generally this śāstra is a commentary on all of the words of the Conqueror, it places particular emphasis on explaining the Mahāyāna. Such a homage also ensures the perfect completion of the translation.

## 3. The text itself

1. Homage and commitment to compose
2. Main exegesis of the text
3. The reason for composing the text

## 1. Homage and commitment to compose

**1**
**To all the Conquerors of the three times, their dharma,**
**And the saṅgha, I pay homage with great devotion.**

What are the objects to which one should pay homage at the beginning of writing a śāstra?

The Buddhas of the ten directions and **the three times** are those who have overcome the dharmas which cause nonvirtue, and are the **all-conquering** victors over the armies of demons resulting from nonvirtue.

**Their dharma** comprises (i) the dharma of words—teachings spoken by the Conqueror and collected in the scriptures, (ii) the dharma of practice—the teachings brought into experience, and (iii) the dharma of realisation—the teachings being fully actualised.

Those who have attained faith through recognising the objects of refuge and virtue, and thus aspire for these and cannot be diverted from them, are **the saṅgha** [Tib. *dge* (virtue), *'dun* (aspiration)]. They dwell on the bhūmis of the śrāvakas in the eight domains of abiding, of the pratyekabuddhas, and of the bodhisattvas.

In one's mind, one perceives the good qualities of taking refuge in these objects and, with one's body and speech, one **pays** them **homage with great devotion**. Such homage is paid by the author in order to complete the composition through the pacification of obscurations and obstructions. In accord with our precious teacher's deed, we, his disciples, should follow suit. Why should we do this? It elevates our ensuing actions.

> **At the urging of my good disciple Changchub-O,**
> **I will shine a lamp of the path to enlightenment.**

This sovereign of the teachings in all of Tibet, this lord of dharma, was born into a noble lineage of bodhisattvas, took ordination and, possessing unwavering faith in the Three Jewels, gazed with the eye of wisdom upon the sūtras and tantras. With great difficulty he brought the Noble Master to Tibet and became his **disciple**, offering everything that could possibly please the master's heart. Thus Lha Lama **Changchub-O,** possessing the **goodness** of exceptional kindness, requested the master to bestow whatever general teachings might be helpful for the Tibetan people at a time when various misunderstandings of the teachings had developed. Thus, **urging** the master, he asked, 'Please compose a śāstra on how to practise, which has few words, condensing the meaning of the entire Mahāyāna'. The master then promised to **shine a lamp** to show the **path to** attain unsurpassed **enlightenment**, expressing his commitment to explain this lamp of the teachings in order that the composition should be completed.

## 2. Main exegesis of the text

1. Analytical summary of the Three Persons
2. Exegesis of the characteristics of each of their paths

## 1. Analytical summary of the Three Persons

2
**Lesser, intermediate and supreme:**
**Thus the Three Persons are to be known.**
**I shall write to clarify the distinctions**
**Between each of their natures.**

How is the path to enlightenment that is referenced in the expression 'I will shine the lamp of the path to enlightenment' to be explained? Although the term 'person' generally indicates a sentient being, here it is synonymous with the Sanskrit term 'puruṣa', which signifies engaging in a function or ability. In this context, the term 'person' means possessing the ability to accomplish the benefit of future lives. One could also use the term 'human' to indicate having a discriminating intellect that is able to discern what to accept and reject for the benefit of future lives. One whose purposes are solely concerned with this life is not therefore what is meant by the terms 'person' or 'human' in this context. As it says in the *Blue Compendium*,[4]

> Afraid of a bad rebirth in the next life, they abandon nonvirtue.
> Wishing to be free from the faults of saṃsāra,
> They practise the three trainings in accord with the Four Noble Truths.
> Afraid of the Hīnayāna, they train in bodhicitta.
> These are the activities of humans.
> There are no other paths than these.

On the path to unsurpassed enlightenment, there is the **lesser** path of the higher realms, the **intermediate** path of ordinary definitive goodness, and the **supreme** path of Buddhahood itself. **Thus the Three Persons are to be known** according to these three paths. **These** paths have their own specific **natures**, **each of** which I shall **distinguish** here by **writing** down and contrasting their differences so that they may be **clearly** or easily understood.

I now present an analytical summary of the general path for those who wish it.[5]

Buddhas, at the outset, generate compassion; in the interim, gather the accumulations; and at the end, attain completely perfect Buddhahood, all solely for the benefit of sentient beings. Thus the entirety of the dharma is given only for the benefit of beings. In regards to this benefit, we may say there are two kinds to be accomplished: temporal happiness and definitive goodness.

All the teachings for the accomplishment of temporal happiness comprise the common dharma cycle of the lesser person. This is a superior kind of lesser person who does not seek improvement within this life but rather strives for the better result of rebirth in the higher realms in the next life, and thus practises the causes of this.

There are two kinds of definitive goodness: the freedom of mere liberation from saṃsāra, and complete omniscience. For the former, one enters the vehicle of the śrāvakas and pratyekabuddhas. All the teachings for this comprise the common dharma cycle of the intermediate person. This type of person, having developed renunciation for all conditioned existence, seeks to accomplish their own individual benefit in the freedom of liberation from conditioned existence, and so enters into the three trainings which are the means for achieving that.

There are two methods for achieving complete omniscience: the Mahāyāna of the perfections and the Mahāyāna of mantras. These two comprise the dharma cycle of the superior person. This type of person, compelled by great compassion, seeks to attain Buddhahood in order to exhaust all the sufferings of all sentient beings and thus trains in the six perfections, the development and completion stages, and so forth.

The main text defines the Three Persons thus:

> Someone using methods by which
> They pursue, for their own good,
> Mere saṃsāric happiness,
> Should be known as inferior.
>
> Someone who turns away from conditioned happiness
> And desists from nonvirtuous actions,
> Seeking only their own individual peace,
> Should be called an intermediate person.
>
> Someone who, by their own suffering,
> Truly wishes to completely end
> All the sufferings of others
> Is a superior person.

The stages of the path of these three kinds of person will be explained below in relation to both the path of the perfections and the path of mantras. The categorisation of the Three Persons is taught in many places, such as Asaṅga's *Yogācārabhūmi Viniścayasaṃgrahanī* and Vasubandhu's *Commentary on the Abhidharmakośa*.

Among those who have attachment to this life and those who are working for the next life, only the latter are 'lesser persons' in the present context, i.e. those who engage in the inerrant methods for attaining the higher states of rebirth. Furthermore although three persons are explained, the path of the greater person contains within it the other two paths, and thus Ācārya Aśvaghoṣa has taught that they are both components of the Mahāyāna path. Therefore the path of the lesser person, which is practised just to attain conditioned happiness, and the path of the intermediate person, which is practised just to attain liberation from saṃsāra for one's individual benefit, together comprise a common path of preliminary practices for the path of the greater person and thus are components of the training of that greater path.

Nevertheless, the essential condition for entering the Mahāyāna is the generation of supreme bodhicitta. As it says in Śāntideva's *Caryāvatāra*,

> The very instant bodhicitta arises
> In someone tormented in the prison of saṃsāra,
> They will be called an 'heir of the Sugatas',
> And be praised by gods and men.

When one develops this intention in one's stream of being, one is called a 'bodhisattva'. Thus to be counted as a Mahāyānist depends upon this intention. Should it be abandoned, one would have left the community of the Mahāyāna. Therefore, one must exert oneself in the various means of developing that intention, fostering feelings of joyfulness in its goodness by meditating on the good qualities of developing it, and practising the seven branch prayer along with taking refuge, as taught in Śāntideva's *Śikṣāsamuccaya* and *Caryāvatāra*. We may summarise the good qualities taught in such texts in terms of temporal happiness and definitive goodness. The former comprises not falling into the lower realms and taking rebirth in the higher realms. When one develops the intention, the causes of lower rebirths one had previously accumulated are purified and its future causes are prevented. Instead, formerly accumulated causes of rebirth in the higher realms are vastly expanded through having this intention and new actions undertaken are made inexhaustible by one's commitment. Finally the resultant good qualities of definitive goodness—liberation and omniscience—will be easily achieved on the basis of this intention.

Is it not natural to wish to achieve these temporal and ultimate benefits? Though someone might think, 'Generating bodhicitta has these good qualities, so I should strive to generate bodhicitta', such bodhicitta would be mere words. In order to develop the proper intention to achieve both the temporal happiness and definitive goodness described above, it is necessary first to stabilise the common attitudes of the lesser and intermediate persons. Then, having developed the desire to attain temporal happiness and definitive goodness, if one wishes to generate the bodhicitta intention to possess the good qualities, one must develop its foundations—loving kindness and compassion. When one considers one's own wanderings in saṃsāra, devoid of happiness and tormented by sufferings, the hairs of one's body should stand on end. Otherwise one will have no feeling for the absence of happiness and the unbearable sufferings of other sentient beings. As it says in the *Caryāvatāra*,

> Those beings never before,
> Even in their dreams,
> Had an intention like this, even for their own sake.
> How could it arise then for the sake of others?

Therefore, one trains as a lesser person by contemplating how one will be afflicted by the sufferings of the lower realms, and as an intermediate person by contemplating how, even in the higher realms, there is only suffering and no happiness. Then, to think of sentient beings who are close to oneself as being subject to experiences like one's own becomes a cause for the development of loving kindness and compassion, from which bodhicitta develops. Thus to practise the contemplations of the lesser and intermediate persons is also a means of developing uncontrived bodhicitta.

Similarly, in both the lesser and intermediate paths, taking refuge, contemplating actions and effects etc. will motivate one to engage in the various means of accumulation and purification. Since the means of purifying one's stream of being—the seven branches, which include the taking of refuge—are also the preliminary practices of bodhicitta, these practices should also be understood in the context of developing the bodhicitta intention. It is important to think of the dharma cycles of the lesser and intermediate persons in this way—as contributing factors of developing bodhicitta—for otherwise they will become separate paths disconnected from the path of the greater person.

How then does one develop genuine bodhicitta in one's stream of being? In order to stabilise the intention, after the preliminary practice of extraordinary refuge, one should perform the ritual of aspiration. After performing this ritual, one should practise the trainings. Develop the wish to train in the conduct of the six perfections, the four means of gathering and so forth. When one has sincerely developed such a wish, one should take the authentic vow of application, after which one's vow must never become impaired by downfalls, even at the risk of one's life. One should also make sure to protect the vow from minor and moderate corruptions, and also from negative actions. However, if the vow is broken, one should apply the authentic methods that have been taught for restoring it. Then one should train in the six perfections in general and, in particular, one should train in meditative absorption, the essence of which is calm abiding, until the mind can be placed for as long as one wishes on a virtuous object. It is taught in the *Lamp of the Path* that one should train in calm abiding in order to develop the higher knowledges, which is one example of its use. The Noble Lord also explains the attainment of calm abiding for the sake of developing higher insight. Thus it is practised for that purpose too. Therefore, in order to sever the bonds of grasping at the two kinds of self, one should unerringly practise meditation to achieve absolute certainty in the view of emptiness, through which one will establish higher insight, the essence of which is discriminating wisdom.

In Atiśa's auto-commentary *Bodhimārgapradīpapañjikā*, it is taught that all the trainings of aspiration and application preceding calm abiding and higher insight comprise the training of moral discipline. Calm abiding is the training of meditation and higher insight is the training of wisdom. Furthermore everything up to and including calm abiding is classified as skilful means, the accumulation of merit, the path of dependence upon relative truth, and the vast graduated path, while generating the three kinds of wisdom is classified as wisdom, the accumulation of primordial wisdom, ultimate truth, and the profound graduated path. Therefore one should develop great certainty that enlightenment will not be attained by disregarding this sequence and classification, separating means from wisdom.

The common path having purified one's stream of being in this way, it is necessary to enter into the mantra vehicle because, when one does so, the two accumulations are swiftly completed. Nevertheless if one does not think that one can do so due to a lack of circumstances, position or ability, one should still begin on the graduated path itself and proceed towards this.

If one enters the mantra vehicle, one should place a special emphasis on the ways of relying upon the spiritual friend, the importance of which is taught in all the vehicles generally but especially so in the mantra vehicle. Then, one's stream of being having been ripened by an empowerment coming from the authentic tantras, one should maintain the vows and pledges taken at that time, even at the risk of one's life. In particular, if one commits a root downfall, then even if one retakes the vow, since its continuity has been broken, it will be difficult to develop the qualities. Therefore one should not violate the vows by committing root downfalls. Do not impair them with branch downfalls either; but should one do so, one should not overlook the infraction but practise confession to purify the vows. Then, train in the elaborate yogas if following the lower tantras and the development stage yogas if following the higher tantras.

Concerning the necessity of developing one's understanding gradually, by way of an example, the Buddha explained in the sūtra of the *Questions of King Dharaṇīśvara* how it is like a skilled jeweller gradually polishing a gem. Furthermore, Lord Nāgārjuna says in the *Ratnāvali*,

> Begin with the qualities of the higher realms,
> And subsequently definitive goodness will arise.
> Then, having attained the higher realms,
> One gradually attains definitive goodness.

Thus he taught that the graduated path proceeds from the higher realms to definitive goodness. Āryadeva says in the *Caryāmelāpakapradīpa*,

> For fortunate beings, from the outset,
> To be able to enter into the sacred meaning,
> The means is, the perfect Buddha has said,
> Like ascending the rungs of a ladder.

## 2. Exegesis of the characteristics of each of the three paths

1. Characteristics of the lesser person's path
2. Characteristics of the intermediate person's path
3. Characteristics of the superior person's path

## 1. Characteristics of the lesser person's path

3
**Someone using methods by which
They pursue, for their own good,
Mere saṃsāric happiness,
Should be known as inferior.**

This is the path of **someone** who is able to accomplish their own benefit for the next life and beyond, without attachment to this life as their main concern. Concerning **the methods** for doing this, having previously developed conviction in karmic causes and results, this person adopts the moral discipline of abandoning the ten nonvirtuous actions, and cultivates the conditioned meditative absorptions, formless meditative absorptions and so forth, known as the 'Deva-yāna' or 'Brahmā-yāna'. By the **use** of such methods **they pursue, for their own good**, the happiness of the highest stage of human existence—the universal emperor—and the **mere saṃsāric happiness** from the level of Indra up to the realms of formlessness. Such a person disregards the benefit of others and pursues conditioned existence, and so is inferior to the intermediate and great person. Thus

**they should be known as inferior** in the context of this teaching. Although in general there are also inferior people who pursue merely the benefits of this life, this too requires engagement in the proper methods of temporal happiness, no different to the inferior person mentioned here.

The method of reliance upon the teacher is the root of the entirety of the path of the Three Persons. If one properly relies on the teacher, then one will develop a wish to utilise the freedoms and endowments of one's precious human birth. But without developing the wish to utilise the basis of freedom and endowment, and practise the holy dharma, there is no point in engaging in any of the paths of the Three Persons.

Since reliance on the teacher and the two dharma cycles of freedom and endowment are the preliminary practices of the path, if one is to practise these instructions, one should first undertake the methods of i) reliance on the teacher and so forth in the proper order. Subsequently, to develop the motivation of the lesser person, one should ii) contemplate impermanence and the faults of the three lower realms. Then, to accomplish the practices, one must iii) take refuge. Then after having contemplated actions and their results, one must iv) train in the moral conduct of abandoning the ten nonvirtues. In the context of this teaching, these four successive dharma cycles comprise the main practices of the path of the lesser person.

## 2. Characteristics of the intermediate person's path

**4**
**Someone who turns away from conditioned happiness
And desists from nonvirtuous actions,
Seeking only their own individual peace,
Should be called an intermediate person.**

By contemplating the innumerable ways in which the entirety of cyclic existence, from the unendurable hell realm to the peak of conditioned existence, is characterised by suffering, one will have no desire for the happiness even of universal emperors, kings and so forth, even in one's dreams. One will **turn away from** all forms of **conditioned happiness and** feel only revulsion for them. This is the contemplative principle of the intermediate path. Motivated by this contemplation, one will **desist from nonvirtuous actions** of body, speech and mind, perfectly maintaining the discipline of whichever one of the seven kinds of prātimokṣa precepts is appropriate. This is the practical principle. On the basis of both the contemplative and practical principles, **someone** who **seeks** nirvāṇa, which is the total **pacification** of all suffering, **only** for their **own individual** self, has the principle of the result. Having these three principles, by entering the path of unerringly practising the holy dharma, one becomes the kind of **person** referred to in this verse.

Being disillusioned with the entirety of conditioned existence, they are better than the lesser person but, because they do not have the altruistic wish to work for the benefit of beings, they are inferior to the supreme person. Therefore such a person **should be called 'intermediate'**.

The intermediate person referred to in the root text may be further distinguished according to their vehicle—that of the śrāvakas and pratyekabuddhas, or according to their object of meditation—the Four Noble Truths or the Twelve Links of Dependent Origination in forward and reverse order. One may also classify intermediate persons into (i) inferior intermediate persons who, with their mind set upon liberation for their own sake, train in the moral discipline of the ten virtues, (ii) middling intermediate persons who, with the same intention, meditate upon the Four Noble Truths, and (iii) superior intermediate persons who, also with that intention, meditate upon the non-self which is empty of duality.

Concerning this, those who follow the most noble Nāgārjuna and Śrī Candrakīrti say there are three kinds of non-self that they meditate upon: (i) the non-self which is merely the emptiness of a substantial individual, (ii) the non-self of dharmas in which one perceives the emptiness of external objects in the conglomerations of partless atoms, and (iii) individuals and dharmas being mere conceptual projections, the subtle non-self which is the emptiness of a truly established intrinsic nature.

Therefore, there are three kinds of understanding and meditation for the person of the Hīnayāna.[6]

According to Sharawa, the main practice on the path of the intermediate person is to 'turn away from conditioned happiness'—the truth of suffering, 'from nonvirtuous actions'—the truth of its origin, 'seeking only one's own individual peace'—the truth of cessation, and 'to desist' from nonvirtue—the truth of the path. Thus the path of the Four Noble Truths, because it also contains within it the Twelve Links of Dependent Origination, is the principal object of meditation for those who want liberation, and is the main practice of the path of the intermediate person.

Furthermore, those who seek liberation should make certain of the two determinations: the first two truths of origination and suffering—the cause which binds and the result of being bound, and the latter two truths of cessation and the path—that which is to be attained and the means of attaining it.

Furthermore, the truth of suffering is to be taught first. Those who want liberation should first meditate thoroughly upon the general and specific faults of saṃsāra to develop an uncontrived longing for liberation. Having developed concern through contemplating the sufferings of saṃsāra, they should then contemplate the causes of saṃsāra. Having seen that saṃsāra is established from defilements and contaminated actions, they should then develop a wish to abandon its source, so the truth of origination is taught next. Meditating on the gradual arising of saṃsāra, they should understand the basis of its origination is unawareness, which is the holding of mistaken views about the nature of objects. When they understand it is possible to abandon such views, they see the possibility to actualise cessation, so the truth of cessation is the next teaching. Then they see that cessation depends upon the path, so the truth of the path is then taught. Maitreya says in the *Uttaratantraśāstra*,

> Just as the disease needs to be diagnosed, its cause eliminated,
> A healthy state achieved, and the remedy implemented,
> So also suffering, its causes, its cessation and the path
> Are to be known, removed, attained and undertaken.

### 3. Characteristics of the superior person's path

1. Brief summary
2. Detailed explanation

### 1. Brief summary

**5**
**Someone who, by their own suffering,**
**Truly wishes to completely end**
**All the sufferings of others**
**Is a superior person.**

An individual who has thoroughly trained their mind on the paths of the lesser and intermediate persons and perfected those trainings will see that throughout the beginning, middle and end, their existence is afflicted **by their own** saṃsāric **suffering**. When such a person contemplates **the sufferings** of all **other** sentient beings as if they were his or her own mothers, thinking of them drifting through an ocean of conditioned existence characterised by such suffering, they become motivated by a compassion which cannot bear that all such beings are tortured, like themselves, by the flames of all these sufferings. Such a person **truly wishes to completely end** all of those sufferings, as well as their causes—the two obscurations together with their karmic imprints—utterly and irreversibly. This is **someone who** has the precious intention to achieve enlightenment with an accompanying wish to work for the benefit of others and, with this motivation, maintains the various kinds of bodhisattva conduct. Since they enter into the inerrant means of accomplishing the Mahāyāna, they have the **superior** or great characteristics mentioned in this verse.

They may be further distinguished according to their view—the Middle Way or Mind Only, according to their vehicle—that of the sūtras or mantras, or according to the swiftness of the path—travelling by ox-drawn cart or by a faster conveyance, etc.

## 2. Detailed explanation of the characteristics of the superior person's path

1. Extensive explanation of the path of the perfections

    2. Brief explanation of how to practise the mantra vehicle

## 1. Extensive explanation of the path of the perfections

    1. Analytical presentation of the path
    2. Analytical presentation of the result

## 1. Analytical presentation of the path

    1. The commitment to explain
    2. Explanation of the authentic path

## 1. The commitment to explain

**6**
**For those excellent beings**
**Who want supreme enlightenment,**
**I will now explain the authentic means**
**Which has been taught by the lamas.**

The expression '**I will now explain**' indicates the forthcoming explanation. What is going to be explained? The indispensable **means** for achieving unsurpassed enlightenment. Who is the explanation **for**? It is for **those excellent beings who** are of the awakened Mahāyāna family and who have the completely pure motivation of **wanting** to attain the level of **supreme enlightenment** for the benefit of others. What kind of explanation is it? It is one without personal fabrication, i.e. it follows that **which has been taught by** holy **lamas** such as the Noble Lord himself and his teacher Serlingpa and, since it possesses scriptural authority and reasoning, is **authentic**. The first two lines identify the vessel for whom the dharma is given. The last two lines identify the nectar-like dharma itself. Furthermore:

- The 'authentic means' is the *explanandum*
- To 'now explain' this is the immediate purpose
- To achieve 'supreme enlightenment' is the meta-purpose
- That 'which has been taught by the lamas' indicates the essential quality of the *explanans*. The meta-purpose depends upon this *explanans*, so their relation is easily understood.[7]

Furthermore, concerning the following lines:

> 'I will shine the lamp of the path to enlightenment.' [Verse 1]

> 'I shall write to distinguish
> Each of their characteristics.' [Verse 2]

> 'I will now explain the authentic means.' [Verse 6]

If these all constitute a commitment to compose, one might object, is this not unnecessary repetition? There is no such fault here. The first is a general commitment to compose a text; the second is a commitment to explain the specific characteristics of the paths of the Three Persons, and the third is a commitment to explain the inerrant means of accomplishing unsurpassed enlightenment for those who belong to the Mahāyāna. Thus one should understand these three statements as distinct. Furthermore, this sixth verse may be taken as a brief statement of what is to follow in the text.

## 2. Explanation of the authentic path

1. Aspiration and its training
2. Application and its training

## 1. Aspiration and its training

This section concerns how students are to train in:

1. Preparations
2. The main practice
3. Subsequent practices

## 1. Preparations

1. Gathering the accumulations
2. The act of going for special refuge
3. Training the mind

## 1. Gathering the accumulations

**7**
**Before an image of the perfect Buddha,**
**A stupa, and the holy dharma,**
**Make offerings with whatever you have—**
**Flowers, incense, materials etc.**

**8**
**With the seven point offering taught in** *Samanthabhadra's Prayer for Good Conduct,*

Before which objects should one make offerings? A representation **of the perfect Buddha** Śākyamuni, such as a painted **image**, bas-relief, or moulded statue as a support of his kāya, **a stupa** housing relics as a support of his mind, **and** a text of the **holy dharma** comprising the twelve scriptural branches etc. as a support of his speech. Having situated oneself directly **before** these objects, one should make offerings. Geshe Sharawa has taught that one should also make prostrations.

What are the substances to be offered? One should offer **material** objects that please the senses—**flowers, incense**, lamps, fragrance and food. Is it sufficient to offer just these pleasing objects? One should offer **whatever one has** without holding anything back for oneself. The Noble Lord himself once said,

> If one has a measure of rice, to give it away is the excellent mind of bodhicitta. Not to give it away is not the excellent mind of bodhicitta.

Thus one should make offerings by actually arranging such physical substances. Geshe Potowa said,

> Offerings should be made of that which most beloved to one. One must do this without the least irritation.

What should be in one's thoughts when making offerings? One should make **the seven point offering** which is **taught in** ***Samanthabhadra's*** *Aspiration Prayer for Good Conduct,* i.e. prostration, offering, confession, rejoicing, requesting, supplicating and dedicating. The term 'offering' applies to all seven of these, because an offering is something that is pleasing, and these seven are particularly pleasing to the recipients.

## 2. The act of going for special refuge

**Until one's destination, the heart of enlightenment, is reached,**
**With the pure intention never to stop,**

**9**
**Have strong faith in the Three Jewels**
**And, placing one knee on the ground,**
**With one's palms together,**
**Begin by going for refuge three times.**

The specific *duration* for special refuge is **until one's destination, the heart of enlightenment, is reached**, i.e. for as long as one has not attained the dharmakāya. The heart of enlightenment has two aspects: a domain and realisation. There are two domains of the heart of enlightenment—the vajra seat of the nirmāṇakāya, and the Densely Arrayed

Akaniṣṭha Buddha field of the saṃbhogakāya. The omniscient master Buton described the realisation of the heart of enlightenment as 'the unsurpassed primordial wisdom of the dharmakāya'.

The specific *motivation* is great compassion which takes all sentient beings as its object. **With** this **pure** and resolute **intention,** one will **never stop** holding the Three Jewels as one's refuge.

The specific *objects* are the **Three** rare and precious **Jewels** of the Buddha—who has attained ultimate abandonment and realisation, the dharma—comprising scripture and realisation, and the saṅgha—the extraordinary community of non-returning noble bodhisattvas.

The specific *attitude* is the fierce **faith** which is **strongly** resolute. This develops with a keen enthusiasm when one hears the special qualities of the Three Jewels. One should adopt a bodily posture with one's legs, **placing one knee on the ground** or sitting up straight, as appropriate **and, with** one's hands, placing **one's palms together**.

The ritual for the main practice of **going for refuge** is **the beginning** of the ritual for generating aspiration bodhicitta. These words of refuge should be recited **three times**. After the third time, one will have taken the vow of refuge. Sharawa said,

> Do not go to the śrāvakas for refuge. Though their blessings are not small, its unsuitability

> is like taking as one's companions those
> travelling a different path.

Also, the *Mahāyānasūtrālaṃkāra* says,

> Because it protects from harms of all kinds,
> The lower realms, unskilful methods,
> Mistaken views and lesser vehicles,
> It is the highest refuge.

The refuge of the lesser person protects them from the harms of this life, the lower realms of the next life, and the unskilful methods of incorrect paths. The intermediate person's refuge frees them from the saṃsāric suffering which is in the nature of the conditioned existence of the mistaken views of the defiled skandhas. To go for special refuge in the Three Jewels is taught as the refuge of the Mahāyāna, because it gives protection from the lesser vehicles, and protects all sentient beings from fears of saṃsāra.

One might then wonder what is the difference between special refuge and aspiration bodhicitta. Potowa said,

> Aspiration is the wish to attain Buddhahood
> for the benefit of sentient beings so that,
> after having attained Buddhahood, one may
> liberate them, like a merchant who travels
> independently. Special refuge is wishing to
> liberate sentient beings from their suffering
> by calling upon the power of the Three

> Jewels, like a merchant who, in dependence
> upon others, travels with guides.

The *Mahāyānasūtrālaṃkāra* says,

> The one who wishes for this object makes a commitment.
> This feeling comes from loving compassion.

Thus it is taught that someone who wishes for Buddhahood makes a commitment or vow. The cause, object, nature, training and benefits of going for refuge should be understood from other sources.

### 3. Training the mind

> **10**
> **Then, a loving intention towards**
> **All sentient beings is the preliminary**
> **To looking upon all beings, without exception,**
> **Suffering throughout the three lower realms,**
> **Birth, death, transmigration etc.**
>
> **11**
> **And wishing to set them free**
> **From the sufferings that torment them,**
> **From suffering, suffering, and its cause.**

After one has completed the act of special refuge, which precedes the gathering of the accumulations, **then** it is necessary to have **a loving intention** which considers **all sentient beings** as one's own mothers, for this **is the preliminary** practice which is the true cause of compassion, being among the seven sequential instructions on cause and effect,[8] as follows. By means of i) recognising all sentient beings as one's mothers, ii) remembering their kindness, and iii) having gratitude for their kindness, an unstable feeling of iv) love and kindness arises. Then one meditates on v) compassion, thinking of their intense **suffering throughout the three lower realms** and how long that lasts for; of the sufferings of **birth**, old age, sickness and **death etc.** that afflict humans; of the sufferings of death, **transmigration** and falling below, which afflict the desire realm gods; and, among the gods of the form and formless levels, one thinks of the sufferings of intoxication by meditative stability, due to which they have no interest in dharma, and thus their meditative stability does not grant them liberation.

In short, one should **look** with the eye of compassion **upon all beings without exception** who are variously tormented by the three kinds of suffering—the **sufferings** of the three lower realms **that torment them**, the **suffering** of change among humans and desire realm gods, and the **suffering** of conditionality among the higher gods. Having considered these **and** considered their origination or root **cause**, actions and defilements, one must strive in fostering a feeling of compassion that **wishes** all those beings **to be set free from** these sufferings.

Then vi) the superior resolution to attain the great enlightenment develops from that. As it says in the *Dharmasamgiti Sūtra*,

> Bodhisattvas should not train in many dharmas. They should train in just one. Which one? Great compassion.

## 2. The main practice

**One should generate bodhicitta,
Which is an irreversible commitment.**

Having thoroughly developed the feelings of loving kindness and compassion in this way, by means of making **an irreversible commitment** never to turn away from the precious mind of enlightenment, **one should generate** the precious **bodhicitta**.

Furthermore, until one has achieved enlightenment, having performed the ritual of aspiration bodhicitta and without deviating from this intention even for an instant, one must be sure to train in the five trainings explained below.

One can learn from other sources how to perform the ritual of aspiration bodhicitta, such as Candragomin's *Twenty Verses*.

## 3. Subsequent practices

1. Training in remembering the benefits
2. Training in the cultivation of bodhicitta

3. Training in gathering the two accumulations
4. Training in not abandoning sentient beings in one's thoughts
5. Training in accepting and rejecting black and white dharmas

## 1. Training in remembering the benefits

**12**
**That is the pure mind of aspiration.**
**The qualities of developing it**
**Have been well explained by Maitreya**
**In the** *Gaṇḍavyūha Sūtra.*

**That** which was explained above **is the pure mind of aspiration** bodhicitta. **The qualities** or benefits **of developing it** through a ritual are limitless. As it says **in the** *Noble Gaṇḍavyūha Sūtra,*

> Son of Noble Family, bodhicitta is like a seed of the qualities of all the Buddhas. It is like a field which makes the white dharmas of all sentient beings thoroughly prosper…

Thus the regent **Maitreya** thoroughly and **well explained** these qualities to the bodhisattva Sudhana through over two hundred examples.

## 2. Training in the cultivation of bodhicitta

**13**
**One should read the sūtras or hear them from the lama,**

**For truly to understand the limitless qualities
  of the mind of perfect enlightenment
Will cause its stabilisation.
Again and again develop the intention in this
  way.**

The **one** for whom bodhicitta has been engendered in the ritual of aspiration bodhicitta referred to above **should read the sūtras** and śāstras **or**, alternatively, properly **hear them from the lama**. There are **limitless** and immeasurable **qualities** or benefits **of the** aspiring **mind** which is intent upon **perfect enlightenment**. These are taught in the basket of Mahāyāna sūtras, etc. and so they should be **truly understood** without uncertainties from such sources. The purpose of doing so is that it **will cause** or bring about the **stabilisation** and unimpeded strengthening of **that** intention in one's stream of being. Thus one should **again and again develop the intention** of bodhicitta **in this way**, at least three times each day and three times each night.

If one does not perform an extensive ritual of bodhicitta, one can recite:

> In the Buddha, the dharma and saṅgha,
> I take refuge until enlightenment.
> By the merit of my practices of giving and so on,
> May I attain Buddhahood for the benefit of all
>   beings.

This verse was written by the Noble Lord himself, so to recite it is a good way of following his example.

**14**
**In the *Sūtra of Vīradatta's Questions***
**Its merit is explained fully.**
**There, in just three of its verses,**
**It is summarised, which I will now quote.**

One might wonder where it is taught that the qualities of bodhicitta are limitless. It comes from the ***Sūtra of the Householder Vīradatta's Questions***, wherein the **merit** and benefits of bodhicitta are **explained** very extensively and **fully. There,** in that sūtra, **in just three of its verses,** the **summary** of this merit **is** explained, so **I will now quote** them here in the main text.

**15**
**"What merit there is in bodhicitta,**
**If it could have form,**
**Would fill the realms of space,**
**And overflow even from this."**

**What**ever **merit there is in** the generation of supreme **bodhicitta,** though it has no form, **if it could have** a **form,** it **would fill or** permeate all **the realms of space** entirely, throughout the ten directions. Such benefit would also **overflow even from this,** for not even space itself could contain it.

**16**
**"However many grains of sand there may be in
The Ganges, as many Buddha fields
Could be completely filled with gems
And offered by someone to the lords of the world,"**

Alternatively, the container is **as many Buddha fields** as the number of **grains of sand there may be in** the shores of the river **Ganges,** or **however many** minute water particles are in the river itself. The basis is **someone** who possesses faith. The offering substance is **to fill them completely** with divine **gems** and wish-fulfilling jewels. The recipients are the **lords of the world**, the Bhagavān Buddhas, to whom the **offerings** are made.

**17**
**"But, if someone folds their hands
With devotion for enlightenment,
Their veneration is superior,
For there is no limit to that."**

**But if** the subject is **someone** who belongs to the Mahāyāna family, and this person should **fold their hands** with faith before the Three Jewels or before the lama **with devotion for** unsurpassed, supreme **enlightenment, their veneration** for developing bodhicitta **is superior** to the former person. **The merit in that** bodhicitta **has no limit** and is therefore supreme.

## 3. Training in gathering the two accumulations

**18**
**Having developed true aspiration bodhicitta,
One should always increase it with all kinds
of exertion.**

By means of remembering the benefits and the training as explained in the previous two sections, one will **develop true aspiration bodhicitta. Having** done so, one should gather the accumulation of merit by such means as making offerings to the Three Jewels, offering service and respect to the saṅgha, giving tormas to spirits and giving alms to the poor. One should also gather the accumulation of primordial wisdom. Thus it is essential to make **all kinds of** such **exertion,** so that the intention of bodhicitta **should always** be **increased.** In Vasubandhu's *Speech on the Accumulations* it says,

> Today I will accumulate merit
> And primordial wisdom. How can I do this?
> What can I do to help others?
> Bodhisattvas consider this again and again.

## 4. Training in not abandoning sentient beings in one's thoughts

In line 18c of the root text, 'In order to remember this as well in other lives', the expression 'as well' has been commented upon by Zhangrompo, who says it means one should also train in the cause of bodhicitta not declining in this life. This is achieved by reflecting, 'I would give up bodhicitta if I abandoned sentient beings in my thoughts'. Some other holy masters have confirmed this to be a good explanation.

## 5. Training in accepting and rejecting black and white dharmas

> **In order to remember this as well in other lives,**
> **Maintain assiduously the trainings just as they are explained.**

Having taken **this** ritual of aspiration bodhicitta referred to above, would it be sufficient just to train in the causes of bodhicitta not declining in this life by practising the four aforementioned trainings? No, that is insufficient. In **other** future **lives**, throughout successive rebirths, **in order to remember** the intention and not forget **it,** one should **maintain assiduously** and keep up **the** four **trainings** in two aspects, white and black, **just as** they are **explained** in the *Sūtra Requested by Kāśyapa*.[9]

## 2. Application and its training

1. Connecting aspiration with the vow of application bodhicitta
2. How one takes the vow
3. Advice on training for one who has taken the vow

## 1. Connecting aspiration with the vow of application bodhicitta

**19**
**Unless one holds the vow of application bodhicitta,**
**Aspiration will not develop to perfection.**
**Those wishing to increase the vow of perfect enlightenment**
**Should definitely make effort to take this vow.**

Although one might generate bodhicitta in this way, if one does not train in the conduct of the Conquerors' sons, enlightenment is impossible. Also, if one does not take the bodhisattva vow, then even if one trains in giving and so forth, that would not constitute the conduct of the Conquerors' sons. Therefore for someone who has stabilised aspiration bodhicitta by the ritual of the vow, it is necessary to then take the vow which is the basis of conduct.

**Unless one holds the vow of application bodhicitta, aspiration** bodhicitta **will not develop** further **to** supreme **perfection.** Therefore, for **those wishing to increase the vow of** aspiration, the vow which is the cause designated by the name of its objective or result—being intent upon **perfect enlightenment**—and bring it to consummation, it is necessary to take the vow of application. Therefore, because it has this characteristic, one **should, making** the utmost **effort,** without any laziness or hesitation, **definitely take this** vow of application.

## 2. How one takes the vow

1. The recipient of the vow
2. The bestower of the vow
3. The ritual method of taking the vow

## 1. The recipient of the vow

**20**
**Apart from always holding**
**The seven kinds of prātimokṣa,**
**The good fortune of this bodhisattva vow**
**Is not to be found anywhere.**

The basis for taking this vow is the holding of one of **the seven kinds of prātimokṣa** vow, from the upāsaka vows up to the vows of a bhikṣu, as well as abandoning inherent misdeeds in general.[10] This is done **always**—i.e. for as long as one lives. **Apart from holding** this basis, **the good fortune** or viable conditions **of this bodhisattva vow** will **not be found anywhere** and will not obtain, because the bodhisattva vow is for those who are able to bring benefit to others directly or indirectly, which is incompatible with the harming of others.

Should someone die, they are released from their prātimokṣa vows. Therefore one may wonder whether it is suitable as a basis for the bodhisattva vow, which does not cease at death. Naljor Chenpo[11] said,

> Just as an old man uses a stick to get up,
> and then afterwards walks with the stick
> so that he does not fall down, at the outset

one must have the generative basis of the prātimokṣa, and then subsequently, having turned away from the basis of harming others, one must keep the bodhisattva vow until the essence of enlightenment without any violation.

## 21
**Among the seven kinds of prātimokṣa Explained by the Tathāgata, The glorious Brahmā conduct is supreme. The vows of the bhikṣu are to be known thus.**

Are certain classes of prātimokṣa better or worse than the others as a basis for the preservation of the bodhisattva vow? **Among the seven kinds of prātimokṣa explained by the Tathāgata** in the Vinaya, from the vows of an upāsaka through to the vows of a bhikṣu, **the glorious** and wonderful path of the monastic vows of the **Brahmā conduct is supreme**, because one enters thereby completely into the doctrine of the Conqueror. **The vows of the bhikṣu are to be known thus** as the supreme basis of the bodhisattva vow.[12] The *Samādhirāja Sūtra* says,

Among the three, the bhikṣu is supreme.[13]

In that case, when someone holding the prātimokṣa vows takes the bodhisattva vow, does their prātimokṣa transform into the bodhisattva vow or are they adding a second vow? In the commentary of Naktso Lotsawa, it says,

One may ask whether the two are the same or distinct vows. They are partly the same and partly distinct. The moral conduct of the vow is to maintain whichever of the seven kinds of prātimokṣa one has taken, and there are no separate practices for the moral conduct of the bodhisattva. In this respect the vows are the same. Yet there are also differences, for the prātimokṣa has a material basis and, having rejected harming others, one does no harm, whereas the bodhisattva vow has no material basis and one must always accomplish the benefit of others. In this respect they are distinct.

## 2. The bestower of the vow

**22**
**One should know the excellent lama**
**To be learned in the ritual of the vow,**
**To be someone who keeps the vow,**
**And to consent to bestow the vow with compassion.**[14]

There are four qualities which **one should know the excellent lama** to have:

> 1. He completely understands and is **learned in** the means of conducting **the ritual of the** bodhisattva **vow**, in holding the vow without breaking it and in restoring the vow if it is broken.

2. He is **someone who** completely **keeps** the moral conduct of **the** bodhisattva **vow**.
3. He is fully able or confident **to consent to bestow** the bodhisattva **vow**.
4. He is completely motivated by **compassion**.

### 3. The ritual method of taking the vow

1. The ritual when the lama is present
2. The ritual when the lama is absent

### 1. The ritual when the lama is present

**23**
**Using the ritual taught in the chapter**
**On moral discipline in the *Bodhisattvabhūmi*,**
**Take the vow from the excellent lama**
**Who possesses the requisite characteristics.**

**The ritual** of the bodhisattva vow **is taught in the chapter on moral discipline** found **in the *Bodhisattvabhūmi*** composed by the noble Asaṅga. **The excellent lama** is someone **who** completely **possesses the requisite characteristics.** One should **take the vow** of application bodhicitta **from** such a lama by completing its preliminary, main and concluding stages, as follows.

In brief, the seven steps of the preliminary are (i) supplication, (ii) enthusiasm, (iii) gathering accumulations, (iv) requesting, (v) generating the special intention, (vi) asking about common obstacles, and (vii) training. The main part comprises promising three times to take on the trainings of all the Buddhas and bodhisattvas of the ten directions and the three times. The five steps of the conclusion are (i) supplicating the omniscient ones, (ii) stating the benefits of entering within the sight of wisdom, (iii) not speaking about the vow without consideration, (iv) briefly stating the training, and (v) making an offering in gratitude.

## 2. The ritual when the lama is absent

1. General and specific commitments to explain this in accord with the tradition
2. Showing how to generate bodhicitta and take the vow as it is taught in the sūtra

## 1. General and specific commitments to explain this in accord with the tradition

**24**
**For one who has tried but been unable**
**To find such a qualified lama,**
**I shall properly explain another ritual**
**To take the vow.**

Although **one** may **have tried** very hard to meet **a lama** who is **qualified** with **such** requisite characteristics to bestow the vow in the manner explained above, one may nevertheless have **been** completely **unable to find** such a one due to certain conditions of place and time. What then is to be done? There is, for this specific circumstance, **another ritual,** besides the ritual for the lama being present, in which one may take the vow by oneself. This ritual for **taking the vow** when the lama is absent **I shall** here **properly explain** in accord with the teachings of the tradition. This constitutes the general commitment to explain the ritual.

**25**
**In a past age, Mañjuśrī,**
**When he was Ambarāja,**
**Generated bodhicitta in the way**
**That is taught in the sūtra of**
***The Ornament of Mañjuśrī's Buddha Realm,***
**As I shall now relate here in full.**

Where is this tradition taught? **In a past age**, innumerable kalpas ago, **Mañjuśrī was** the universal emperor **Ambarāja**, whose name means 'King of the Skies'. In the presence of the Tathāgata called 'King of the Song of Thunder', **he generated** unsurpassed **bodhicitta in the way that is taught in the sūtra of** *Showing the Ornamental Display of Mañjuśrī's Buddha Realm.* **I shall now relate here** what is taught in that text **in full**. This constitutes the specific commitment to explain the ritual.

## 2. Showing how to generate bodhicitta and take the vow as it is taught in the sūtra

1. Generating bodhicitta
2. Taking the vow

## 1. Generating bodhicitta

**26**
"In the presence of the Protectors,
I generate perfect bodhicitta.
Inviting all beings as my guests,
I will liberate them from saṃsāra."

**The Protectors** of all sentient beings are the enlightened Buddhas, **in the presence of** whom **I generate** the completely **perfect,** unsurpassed **bodhicitta**. For this purpose, **all beings** without exception, reaching to the ends of space, I **invite as my guests,** i.e. **I will** bring benefit to them, **liberating them from** the saṃsāric rivers of suffering, which they have not crossed over, and unlocking the chains of the origination of suffering, from which they have not been freed. With the truth of the path, I will expel the breath of the view of self for those who have not expelled it, and with the truth of cessation I will place in nirvāṇa, the transcendence of torment, those who have not transcended the torment of dualistic grasping. Therefore this way of presenting the invitation of guests in terms of the Four Noble Truths is explained by Sharawa as a practice of both aspiration and application.

## 2. Taking the vow

1. Adopting the moral conduct of avoiding violations of the vow
2. Adopting the moral conduct of benefitting sentient beings

3. Adopting the moral conduct of gathering virtuous dharmas

## 1. Adopting the moral conduct of avoiding violations of the vow

**27**
**"From now until I have attained**
**Perfect enlightenment, I will cease**
**Intentions of harm, aggression,**
**Greed and envy."**

**From now**, this day, for as long as **I have** not yet **attained** unsurpassed **perfect enlightenment,** I promise to **cease** the following four intentions. **Intentions of harm,** such as wanting to kill out of hatred, arise in dependence upon the various causes of malicious thought. **Aggression** is sudden outbursts of anger towards others. **Greed** is an inability to give things away to others. **Envy** is dissatisfaction with the prosperity of others.

**28**
**"I will practise pure conduct**
**And abandon nonvirtue and desire.**
**Taking joy in the vow of conduct,**
**I will train following the Buddhas."**

**I will practise the pure conduct** of giving up sexual activity, **and** I will **abandon nonvirtuous** actions and the attachment to objects of **desire** which cause them. **Taking joy in the** completely pure **vow of conduct** to abandon these, **I will** properly **train following** the sublime conduct of **the Buddhas.**

## 2. Adopting the moral conduct of benefitting sentient beings

> **29**
> "Taking no pleasure in swiftly
> Attaining enlightenment for myself,
> I will remain until the end
> For even a single being."

**Taking no pleasure** and feeling no joy **in** the intention **swiftly** to **attain enlightenment for myself, I will remain** for as long as saṃsāra has not reached its final **end for** the benefit of **even a single being.**

## 3. Adopting the moral conduct of gathering virtuous dharmas

> **30**
> "I will utterly purify
> Inconceivable fields without limit.
> For those who remember my name,
> I will remain for them throughout the ten directions."

One may ask what is to be practised after the foregoing has been stabilised. One should **utterly purify inconceivable** Buddha **fields** of imperfections such as ravines, briars and so forth, **without** any graspable **limit**. With the wish to bring benefit to **those** beings **who** hear one's **name** and **remember** it, or who see, hear, remember or touch one, by means of one's fame **throughout** the realms of all **the ten directions,** and by **remaining** there **for them,** one will purify and ripen the worlds of sentient beings.

**31**
**"I will purify entirely**
**Actions of body and speech.**
**I will purify the activity of mind too,**
**And I will cease nonvirtuous actions."**

For beginners it is necessary to emphasise the moral conduct of maintaining one's vows. Therefore one should repeat the following words. **"I will purify entirely,** without the stain of downfalls, the **actions of body and speech,** and **I will purify the activity of mind** from downfalls **too.** In short, until enlightenment has been attained in all its aspects, **I will** always **cease nonvirtuous actions** of the three gates."

*[End of '2. How one takes the (application) vow']*

## 3. Advice on training for one who has taken the vow

1. Training of moral conduct
2. Training of mind
3. Training of wisdom

## 1. Training of moral conduct

1. The actual training
2. Its great importance

## 1. The actual training

**32**
**If one keeps the vow of application bodhicitta,
It is the cause of complete purification of body, speech, and mind.
If the moral conduct of the three trainings is properly practised,
Devotion to the moral conduct of the three trainings will grow greater.**

What is the cause of the purification of the three gates? The *subject* of purification is the bodhisattva, the **one** who belongs to the Mahāyāna family and who **keeps the vow of application bodhicitta**. The *purpose* of so doing **is** to **cause** the **complete purification of** downfalls from their own **body, speech and mind** and to train in the causes of the supreme benefit of other sentient beings. The *object* is **the moral conduct of the three trainings**. If one trains with diligence and in the **proper** manner, by the power of one's **practice**, one's **devotion,** by which one holds with great reverence **the moral conduct of the three** previously mentioned **trainings, will grow greater.**

The term 'proper' here has three senses—purity, irreversibility and completeness. Proper training in the moral conduct of the vow is *pure* like the beautiful form of a holy person. Proper training in the moral conduct of benefitting others is *irreversible* and without corruption like being completely free of disease. Proper training in the moral conduct of gathering virtuous dharmas is *complete* like a pot filled to the brim.

Furthermore the term 'great bodhisattva [Tib. *byang chub kyi sems dpa' chen po*]' is derived from the three trainings—the moral conduct of the vow purifies [*byang*] all faults; the moral conduct of gathering virtuous dharmas accomplishes [*chub*] all qualities, and the moral conduct of benefitting others transforms one into a great hero [*sems dpa' chen po*].

## 2. Its great importance

**33**
**Therefore, intent upon pure and perfect**
  **enlightenment,**
**Bodhisattvas will keep the vow of vows pure.**
**They will endeavour in perfect enlightenment**
**And completely fulfill the accumulations.**

One's body, speech and mind will be purified by training in the three kinds of moral conduct. **Therefore,** the complete **purification** of what is to be abandoned **and** the absolute **perfection** of the antidotes results in unsurpassed **enlightenment**. The **bodhisattvas** who are **intent upon** or focussed upon achieving this for the benefit of others **will keep pure** or maintain **the vows** of the three kinds of moral conduct, among which the moral conduct **of** the **vow** is the most important. By means of mindfulness, clear comprehension and concern, they **will endeavour** diligently and with great dedication in the causes of **perfect enlightenment**—the two **accumulations** of merit and wisdom—and **will completely fulfill** these.

*[End of '1. Training of moral conduct']*

## 2. Training of mind

1. That training in calm abiding is the cause of developing the higher knowledges
2. How to train in calm abiding

### 1. That training in calm abiding is the cause of developing the higher knowledges

**34**
**The cause of completely perfecting the accumulations,**
**The natures of which are merit and wisdom,**
**Is held by all the Buddhas**
**To be the development of the higher knowledges.**

Therefore, **the** specific **cause of completely perfecting** and bringing to fulfilment **the** two **accumulations, the natures of which are merit and wisdom, is held by all the Buddhas** of the three times **to be the development of the** six **higher knowledges.**

**35**
**Just as a bird with unfledged wings**
**Cannot fly in the sky,**
**So, without the power of the higher knowledges,**
**One cannot benefit beings.**

Accomplishing the benefit of beings also depends on the higher knowledges. **Just as,** for example, **a bird with wings** that are **not** yet fully **fledged cannot fly in the sky, so** accordingly **without the power of the higher knowledges, one cannot** bring vast **benefit** to **beings** in accordance with their individual circumstances.

In the *Mother of the Perfection of Wisdom in Eighteen Thousand Lines Mahāyāna Sūtra* it says,

> Subhūti, for example, without wings, a bird cannot fly in the sky. Similarly, without relying upon the higher knowledges, a bodhisattva cannot teach the dharma to sentient beings. Since he will lead them in the wrong direction, he cannot take sentient beings along the path.

Regarding the higher knowledges, with (i) the higher knowledge of miracles, one can travel to the realms of Buddhas and to realms where there are beings to be trained. With (ii) the knowledge of others' minds, one knows exactly their character and thoughts. With (iii) the divine ear, one understands their languages. With (iv) the knowledge of previous lives, one knows the prior causes of present lives. With (v) the divine eye, one knows their futures. With (vi) the knowledge of cessation of corruption, one knows their inclinations towards the three vehicles leading to enlightenment and liberation, and by which of these they will be ripened and liberated.

**36**
**Whatever merit may be obtained in a single day
By someone endowed with the higher knowledges,
Will not be obtained in a hundred lifetimes
By someone who lacks them.**

Furthermore, **whatever** accumulation of **merit may be obtained** or gathered **in a single day by someone** for whom bodhicitta is **endowed with the higher knowledges**, that merit **will not be obtained** even **in a hundred lifetimes by someone who lacks them,** even though they may be the same in respect of having generated bodhicitta. This also applies to the accumulation of wisdom.

**37**
**Those who want to complete swiftly
The accumulations of perfect enlightenment
Will accomplish the higher knowledges
Not through laziness but through effort.**

One may ask what is the essential cause of the higher knowledges. For **those who want to complete the** two **accumulations swiftly**, which are the causes **of** attaining **perfect enlightenment**, it is necessary to develop the use of **the higher knowledges**, the cause of which is very vigorous **effort, through** which the six higher knowledges **will** be **accomplished**. However, the higher knowledges will **not** be accomplished by someone with **laziness.** Therefore it is necessary to apply effort.

**38**
**Since without achieving calm abiding
The higher knowledges will not arise,
One should apply oneself again and again
In trying to accomplish calm abiding.**

What should one apply one's effort to? **Since without achieving** genuine **calm abiding** which is suffused with pliancy and complete purity, **the** extraordinary **higher knowledges** which arise from the power of meditation **will not arise, one should apply oneself again and again** in the various means of stabilising the mind, **trying to accomplish** the essential cause of the higher knowledges, which is **calm abiding**.

## 2. How to train in calm abiding

1. The prerequisites of calm abiding
2. How to meditate on calm abiding
3. The benefits of the meditation

## 1. The prerequisites of calm abiding

**39**
**While the conditions of calm abiding are weak,
Even to meditate with strong diligence
For thousands of years
Will not accomplish samādhi.**

**40**
**Therefore, maintain well the conditions
Taught in the *Tract on the Accumulation of Samādhi*.**

Can calm abiding be achieved through diligence alone? No. **While the conditions** or causal prerequisites **of calm abiding are weak, even to meditate with strong diligence** and fierce exertion **for** as long a time as many **thousands of years will not accomplish** the **samādhi** of calm abiding. **Therefore,** because calm abiding will not be achieved if these conditions are weak, one should **maintain well the conditions taught in the** *Tract on the Accumulation of Samādhi*,[15] the *Śrāvakabhūmi* and so forth. By achieving this, samādhi will develop.

## 2. How to meditate on calm abiding

**Place the mind in virtue**
**On any suitable object of attention.**

Therefore, one who maintains the causal conditions for calm abiding should **place the mind** (the subject of meditation) one-pointedly and without distraction **in virtue on any suitable**—i.e. which comes from the sūtras and śāstras—**object of attention** (the object of meditation) that has been taught by the Conqueror.

## 3. The benefits of the meditation

**41**
**When the yogin attains calm abiding,**
**The higher knowledges are attained also.**

**When the yogin** makes effort like the continual flow of a river in the aforementioned samādhi and **attains calm abiding,** not only **are the higher knowledges**

**attained** through such training, but **also** the non-conceptual primordial wisdoms. The Noble Lord himself said in the *Summary of the Accomplishment of the Mahāyāna Path*,

> Because it leads to the power of the higher knowledges
> And the undefiled path,
> One should first develop calm abiding.

*[End of '2. Training of mind']*

### 3. Training of wisdom

1. Showing the training in higher insight by showing the reason for unifying means and wisdom
2. How to train in higher insight

### 1. Showing the training in higher insight

1. The essential point of the need to train in the wisdom of higher insight
2. The essential point of the need to train in unifying means and wisdom
3. Explaining the actual path of unification

### 1. The essential point of the need to train in the wisdom of higher insight

> Yet without the yoga of the perfection of wisdom,
> The obscurations will not be exhausted.

**42**
**Therefore, in order to abandon completely
The obscurations of defilements and cognition,
Cultivate the perfection of wisdom
Always in conjunction with skilful means.**

One may **yet** wonder in that case whether it is sufficient merely to develop calm abiding and the higher knowledges which come from that. Although one may abandon the manifest defilements through ordinary meditative concentrations, since these are **without the yoga** or union **of the perfection of wisdom** that cognises reality itself, one **will not exhaust** the seeds of either of **the** two **obscurations** of defilements and cognition. Mahācārya Candragomin said in the *Praise of Confession*,

> Again and again the forest fire of concentration
> May burn away the many thickets of faults,
> But if the strong roots of self view are not uprooted,
> They will grow back as though watered by rain.

**Therefore,** because of that essential point, **in order to abandon completely the obscurations of** the **defilements**, such as desire, **and** the obscurations of **cognition**—the imprints of deluded dualistic appearances—it is necessary to **always** continually **cultivate** the yoga of **the perfection of wisdom,** which cognises reality itself, **in conjunction with**

**skilful means** such as giving. Śāntideva's *Caryāvatāra* says,

> Emptiness is the antidote to the darkness
> Of the obscurations of defilements and cognition.
> How can those who wish to attain omniscience
> Not hurry to meditate on it?

The first two lines of the root text show that it is impossible to abandon the defilements without the wisdom which comprehends reality itself, which implies that even śrāvakas and pratyekabuddhas have some understanding of emptiness, because they are able to abandon the defilements. The subsequent four lines show that since the greater and lesser vehicles are not differentiated by their view, those travelling on the Mahāyāna path must train in the wisdom which is embraced by vast skilful means.[16]

## 2. The essential point of the need to train in unifying means and wisdom

**43**
**Wisdom without skilful means**
**And skilful means without wisdom**
**Were said to be prisons.**
**Do not therefore abandon either of them.**

Since neither **wisdom** alone **without skilful means** nor **skilful means** alone **without wisdom** will bring about Buddhahood, those who seek perfect enlightenment must train in the path of unifying means and wisdom. The Bhagavān Buddha said in the *Sūtra of the Teaching of Vimalakīrti*,

> Wisdom without skilful means is **a prison**.
> Skilful means without wisdom is a prison.

This being **said**, one should **not therefore abandon** or neglect **either** one **of them.**

### 3. Explaining the actual path of unification

1. Brief summary
2. Detailed explanation

### 1. Brief summary

**44**
**To eliminate doubts concerning**
**What 'wisdom' and 'skilful means' are,**
**I will now clarify the correct distinction**
**Between skilful means and wisdom.**

One may then ask what is the specific nature of each of these? In order **to eliminate** such **doubts,** misunderstandings and false ideas **concerning what 'wisdom' and 'skilful means' are, I will now clarify the correct** and inerrant **distinction** or differentiation **between** the essential characteristics of **skilful means and wisdom**, which may otherwise seem indistinct.

## 2. Detailed explanation

1. Identifying means
2. The necessity of developing it
3. Identifying wisdom

## 1. Identifying means

**45**
**Apart from the perfection of wisdom,**
**All virtuous dharmas,**
**Such as the perfection of giving,**
**Were taught by the Conquerors to be skilful means.**

**Apart from** or excluding **the perfection of wisdom, all** of the **virtuous** white **dharmas** which accomplish bodhicitta, **such as** for instance **the perfection of giving, were taught by the Conquerors** of the three times **to be**long to the category of **skilful means.**

## 2. The necessity of developing it

**46**
**Whoever cultivates wisdom**
**Through the power of cultivating skilful means**
**Will soon attain enlightenment**
**But, by cultivating non-self alone, will not.**

Having begun to meditate upon impermanence, actions and results, **whoever,** a bodhisattva, **cultivates** the **wisdom** which severs the mental habit of objective grasping at the characteristics of whatever is conceived as outer or inner objects, has a very great ability to abandon the obscurations **through the power of** practising very stably the **cultivation** of **skilful means,** such as giving. They **will soon attain** unsurpassed **enlightenment** itself **but,** should they neglect the aspect of means **by cultivating non-self alone,** they **will not** attain unsurpassed enlightenment.

## 3. Identifying wisdom

**47**
**The skandhas, dhātus, and āyatanās**
**Are to be understood as being without arising.**
**This recognition of the emptiness of intrinsic nature**
**Is the definition of 'wisdom'.**

**The** five **skandhas**, eighteen **dhātus, and** twelve **āyatanās** are the thirty-five 'dharmins' or objects [Tib. *dmigs pa*]. The perceptible qualities which are above these are 'dharmas' or qualities [Tib. *rnam pa*]. All of these **are to be understood** or recognised **as being without arising** with an intrinsic nature. The primary cause of wandering in saṃsāra is attachment to the reality of the substantial existence of whatever appears. Moreover, to grasp at arising with an intrinsic nature is itself the basis of all the other grasping at substantial existence. Thus it is necessary to cease that by understanding that there is no arising with an intrinsic nature. Similarly, there is no departing either, as if what formerly arose is subsequently destroyed. Since they have always been empty, **this recognition of the emptiness of the intrinsic nature** of all dharmas, which are to be understood as without arising with an intrinsic nature, **is the definition of 'wisdom'** from among the two terms 'means' and 'wisdom'. This recognition also constitutes the essential training of wisdom.

*[End of '1. Showing the training in higher insight as a way of showing the reason for unifying means and wisdom']*

## 2. How to train in higher insight

1. Detailed explanation
2. Concluding summary

## 1. Detailed explanation

1. The basis for accumulating higher insight
2. How to meditate on higher insight
3. The results of meditating on higher insight

## 1. The basis for accumulating higher insight

1. Showing the wisdom of reflection which arises from analytical contemplation
2. Showing the wisdom of hearing which arises in dependence upon scripture

## 1. Showing the wisdom of reflection which arises from analytical contemplation

1. The analysis of result: the argument of arising and cessation from existence or nonexistence
2. The analysis of cause: the argument of the vajra slivers
3. The analysis of nature: the argument of the one and the many

## 1. The analysis of result: the argument of arising and cessation from existence or nonexistence

**48**
**Arising from existence is not logical,**
**Nor is arising from nonexistence, like a skyflower.**
**Consequently both are errors.**
**Therefore there is no arising from both, either.**

In response to the foregoing definition of wisdom as the recognition of nonarising with intrinsic nature, proponents of substantial existence might say, 'We do not accept this. Objects arise with an intrinsic nature and pass away because they are actually existent.' If that were so, if a sprout arose with an intrinsic nature, then, at the time of its cause, was the sprout existent, nonexistent, both or neither?

1. If the logical subject—the sprout—was existent at the time of its cause, its **arising from** that **existence is not logical,** for its existence would already have

been attained, and so there is no need for it to arise. If something already existent arose again, there would be an infinite regress.

2. If it was **nonexistent** at the time of the cause, to arise **from** that with an intrinsic nature is also not logical, whatever causal powers may occur, because it is impossible for a real sprout with its own intrinsic nature to arise from nothing, **like**, for example, the creation of **a sky flower**. We do not say that in general what is nonexistent at the time of its cause must necessarily remain nonexistent, only that if something with an intrinsic nature is nonexistent at the time of its cause, then that must remain nonexistent in every respect. Furthermore Nāgārjuna in the *Root Verses on the Middle Way* says:

> 'It arose previously but now is nonexistent,'
> Entails the consequence of annihilationism.

3. If both existent and nonexistent, because **consequently both** of the aforementioned positions **are errors, there is no** argument for something **arising** with an intrinsic nature at the time of the cause **from both** existence and nonexistence**, either.**

4. Nor is it acceptable to claim arising from neither, because there is no category of substantial being apart from existence and nonexistence.

Therefore the sprout, the logical subject, does not arise with an intrinsic nature, because whatever has an intrinsic nature cannot have arisen from existence, nonexistence, both or neither. This argument establishes that nonarising is the domain of wisdom. As Nāgārjuna says in the *Seventy Verses on Emptiness,*

> From existent, because existent, it cannot arise.
> From nonexistent, because nonexistent, it cannot arise.
> Because contradictory, not both.
> Because not arising, neither persisting nor ceasing.

## 2. The analysis of cause: the argument of the vajra slivers

**49**
**Objects do not arise from self,**
**Nor from other, nor from both,**
**Nor without cause, because of which,**
**They have no intrinsic nature.**

Outer and inner **objects** are the logical subject. They **do not arise from self**, because their arising would have no purpose and would recur infinitely. Furthermore, as Nāgārjuna says in *Root Verses on the Middle Way,*

> If cause and effect were the same,
> Producer and product would be the same.

**Nor** do they arise with an intrinsic nature **from other**. If the other had its own intrinsic nature, the designated creator and created would have no connection, and therefore anything could arise from anything else. Furthermore the following objection of Nāgārjuna would apply:

> If cause and effect had other intrinsic
> natures,
> Causes would be equivalent to non-causes.

The logic of this argument is the lack of identity of the cause and effect. The identity of the arising and ceasing self has one intrinsic nature and, because of its cessation, is distinct from the arising and ceasing other, which has another intrinsic nature.

**Nor** do they arise **from both** self and other, because the arising from each of these has already been individually refuted.

**Nor** do they arise **without** a **cause.** Since a harvest would arise regardless of agriculture, there would be no point in ordinary people engaging in it. Furthermore as Dharmakīrti says in the *Root Verses Commenting on Logic*:

> Because what is causeless is autonomous,
> It permanently remains existent or
> nonexistent.

Therefore, **because** arising from these four extremes has been shown to be impossible, objects **have no intrinsic nature**.

## 3. The analysis of nature: the argument of the one and the many

> 50
> Or, if all dharmas
> Are analysed for singularity and multiplicity,
> Since no essence is seen,
> It is certain they have no intrinsic nature.

**Or**, in addition to the preceding explanations, another argument may be presented. **All** outer and inner **dharmas** are the logical subject. **If** they are **analysed for** the existence of an inherent intrinsic nature as a **singularity and** as a **multiplicity, no** objectively existent **essence is seen**, not even so much as an atom. **Since** that is the case, **it is certain they have no intrinsic nature,** being like, for example, reflections in a mirror.

## 2. Showing the wisdom of hearing which arises in dependence upon scripture

> 51
> The arguments of the *Seventy Verses on Emptiness,*
> *The Root Verses on the Middle Way* and so forth,
> Show the proofs for the emptiness
> Of the intrinsic nature of things.

In order that intelligent ones may be correctly led towards certainty in profound emptiness, they should study the following texts to resolve all doubts. To establish the definitive meaning of emptiness by scriptural tradition, one should study Nāgārjuna's *Sūtrasamuccaya.* To establish by reasoning **the arguments** for emptiness, one should study the logic of Nāgārjuna's collection of reasonings such as **the *Seventy Verses on Emptiness*** and **the *Root Verses on the Middle Way,*** which definitively establish profound emptiness through many arguments. '**And so forth**' means one should also study the supreme works of Buddhapālita and the most venerable Candrakīrti, which explain the true intent of the Noble Lord Nāgārjuna, and the works of Śāntideva too. These texts **show the proofs for the emptiness of the intrinsic nature of things,** the primordial nature of reality. They should be read thoroughly and their meaning should be decisively understood.

### 52
**Because this text would become too long,**
**I will not elaborate on them here,**
**But I have fully explained just the established tenets**
**For the purpose of meditation.**

That being the case, should the principles of this vast corpus of scripture and reasoning be presented here? Out of concern that **this text would become too long** if that were to be attempted, **I will not elaborate on them here. But** instead of this I **have fully explained just** a condensed summary of **the tenets established** by scripture and reasoning **for the purpose of meditation** upon non-self.

The logic of the great dependent origination is presented in the *Seventy Verses on Emptiness,* which quotes the *Sāgaramati Sūtra,* as follows:

> Whatever arises in dependence and connection,
> Is that which has no essence.[17]

It is clearly taught there that dependent origination refutes the existence of an intrinsic nature. This is also clearly taught in the *Sūtra Requested by the Nāgā King Anavatapta,* which says,[18]

> Whatever arises from conditions is unarisen.
> There is no intrinsic nature in such arising.
> That which depends upon conditions is explained as empty.
> Whoever knows emptiness has concern.[19]

The meaning of the term 'unarisen' in the first line is explained in the second line as there being nothing with an intrinsic nature that arises. The third line explains the term 'empty' as meaning relying upon the dependent connection of assembled conditions. While something dependently originated is taught here as being empty of existence with an intrinsic nature, it is not said that it is empty of performing a function as a mere appearance, the arising of which has been refuted. It says in the *Root Verses on the Middle Way,*

> That which is dependently originated
> Is pacified of an intrinsic nature.

Thus, by the essential characteristic of arising through dependence, there is the 'pacification' or being empty of an established intrinsic nature. The proofs related to such dependent origination in the Middle Way treatises are highly praiseworthy. In the *Sūtra Requested by the Nāgā King Anavatapta* it says,

> The wise come to understand the dependent origination of dharmas,
> Such that they have no need of extreme views.

Thus it is taught that by correctly understanding dependent origination, one will not hold any view in which there is clinging to extremes. This is the unmatched distinguishing feature of the father-son lineage of the great master Nāgārjuna.

There are two main obstacles to or deviations from the correct view:

1. The overstating view of eternalism, in which one objectifies dharmas as the object of grasping
2. The diminishing view of annihilationism, in which, having negated the direct connection in dependent origination from cause to effect, one cannot identify what is and is not a cause of an effect

In dependence upon the syllogism that ascertains the dependent arising of specific effects from specific causes and conditions, the existence of intrinsic nature is refuted, completely refuting both of these errors. The annihilationist view is refuted by ascertaining the meaning of the syllogism's premise [that the object is dependently originated through causes and conditions]. The eternalist view is refuted by ascertaining the meaning of the syllogism's conclusion [that therefore the object does not arise with an intrinsic nature].

Therefore, outer objects such as shoots arise in dependence upon seeds etc., and inner objects such as concepts arise in dependence upon ignorance etc. That being so, their existence with independent characteristics cannot be logically established. If they existed with an independent intrinsic nature, they would exist by their own autonomous power, which is incompatible with their dependence upon causes and conditions. By such logic, one should also understand that persons, vases etc. are designations dependent upon composites, and do not exist with intrinsic natures.

If the arising of these is dependent and their designation is dependent, it does not follow that they exist with the same intrinsic nature as whatever they depend upon. If they had an identical intrinsic nature, all causal agents and their products would be the same. Nor do they exist with different intrinsic natures. If they did, one could deny their causal relations, which would contradict their dependence. As it says in the *Root Verses on the Middle Way*,

> Whatever arises in dependence upon something,
> Is neither identical to that thing,
> Nor something other than it.
> Hence it is neither disconnected nor continuous.

As one ascertains the emptiness that is completely empty of conceptual objects with graspable characteristics, one does not dispense with the ascertainment of relations between actions and results. Thus it is highly praiseworthy to rely upon such correct acceptance and rejection. It says in Nāgārjuna's *Bodhicittavivaraṇa*,

> Having understood the emptiness of dharmas,
> To rely on actions and results
> Is the wonder of wonders;
> The marvel of marvels.

Therefore one must distinguish existing with an intrinsic nature from merely apparent existence, and not existing with essential characteristics from unqualified nonexistence. It says in Candrakīrti's *Autocommentary on Entering the Middle Way*,

> Cognisant of the operation of causes and effects that brings about an essenceless reflection, and having seen that forms, feelings etc., are no different from reflections in their participation in causes and effects, having merely apparent

> existence, what wise person would ascertain
> their inherent existence? Therefore,
> although they might be taken as existent,
> they do not arise with an intrinsic nature.

Thus if such distinctions are not made, one will think that where there is an intrinsic nature, the object exists, and where there is no intrinsic nature, there is nonexistence. Thus one will not transcend the two extremes of overstatement and diminishment. Therefore the nonexistence of intrinsic nature liberates all extremes of existence, and the ability to accept causes and effects without intrinsic nature liberates all extremes of nonexistence.

In short, to take all apparent dharmas as reality, or to take their negated existence and non-establishment as reality, is to fall into the extremes of eternalism and annihiliationism respectively, positions which are contrary to the true nature of things. However, views such as the nonexistence of dharmas in ultimate truth, or the designated existence of causes and effects etc. are not extremes, because the perceived objects are taken as mere appearances. It says in the *Seventy Verses on Emptiness*,

> We do not refute the worldly convention
>   which says,
> 'In dependence upon this, that arises.'

*[End of '1. The basis for accumulating higher insight']*

## 2. How to meditate on higher insight

**53**
**Therefore, whoever meditates upon non-self**
**Without seeing an intrinsic nature**
**Of any dharma whatsoever**
**Is meditating upon wisdom.**

**Therefore** having determined that all dharmas, which are composites of skandhas, dhātus, and āyatanas, are without self, if individuals or **any dharma without** any exception **whatsoever,** such as the skandhas, had an **intrinsic nature**, then one would have discovered it when one searched for it with scripture and reasoning. Yet since one **does not see** as much as an atom with an intrinsic nature, there is **no self** which exists with an intrinsic nature in individuals or dharmas. **Whoever meditates** on this and applies such reasoning **is meditating upon** the perfection of **wisdom.** As it says in the *Bhāvanākrama* of Kamalaśīla,

> Why are all things analysed with wisdom for an intrinsic nature? Because it creates the samādhi of non-seeing, which we call the samādhi of supreme wisdom.

**54**
**Just as one with wisdom does not see**
**Any intrinsic nature in all dharmas,**
**So wisdom itself is subject to analysis.**
**One should meditate without any concepts.**

One may ask how to abandon grasping at a wisdom which involves concepts. **Just as one with** the **wisdom** of conceptual analysis **does not see any** truly existent **intrinsic nature in** the individual or in **all dharmas** when analysed**, so wisdom itself is** also **subject to analytical** investigation in which no truly existent intrinsic nature is found. Being free from singularity and multiplicity, one understands the subjective mind is nonarising, and rests **without any concepts** of it. **One should meditate** with the certainty that this is the cause of non-conceptual wisdom.

## 3. The results of meditating on higher insight

1. The main part
2. Establishing it by scriptural reference

## 1. The main part

**55**
**This world comes from conceptual discrimination.**
**Its very core is conceptual discrimination.**
**Therefore, abandon such discrimination entirely.**
**That is the supreme nirvāṇa.**

The entirety of the foundations of the three realms of **this** saṃsāric **world comes from** the **conceptual discrimination** of clinging to reality. **Its very core is** contrived by **conceptual discrimination. Therefore, abandon** conceptual **discrimination entirely** and without remainder, along with all of its imprints. **That** attainment establishes all benefits of self and other in **the supreme** liberation of non-abiding **nirvāṇa**.

## 2. Establishing it by scriptural reference

**56**
**Thus the Bhagavān said,**
**'Conceptual discrimination is the great ignorance.**
**It plunges one into the ocean of saṃsāra.**
**Resting in non-discriminating samādhi,**
**Sky-like non-discrimination will be revealed.'**

**Thus** one might ask how saṃsāra arises from conceptual discrimination and how it can be abandoned by meditation on non-self. **The Bhagavān said** in the *Saṃpuṭa* tantra that **conceptual discrimination,** the grasping of objects, **is** to be known as **the great ignorance** that is the foundation of conditioned existence, because **its** force **plunges one into the** bottomless and shoreless **ocean of saṃsāra.** When one attains the certainty of the analytical understanding of non-self as the antidote to conceptual discrimination which grasps reality, one **rests in** and cultivates the **non-discriminating samādhi** that is free from the conceptual discrimination of analytical categories. When this meditation is perfected, one **will** clearly see **revealed** the true **non-discriminating** nature of mind which, **like** the **sky**, is free from the obscuring clouds of autumn. As it says in the *Saṃpuṭa* tantra,

> Conceptual discrimination is the great ignorance.
> It plunges one into the ocean of saṃsāra.
> Resting in the non-discriminating samādhi,
> Non-discrimination, like space, will be revealed.

**57**

**In the *Dhāraṇī of Entering into Non-discrimination Sūtra* it likewise says,
'Should sons of the Conquerors meditate upon
This sacred teaching of non-discrimination,
They will escape the disturbances of discrimination,
And gradually achieve non-discrimination.'**

Furthermore **in the *Dhāraṇī of Entering into Non-discrimination Sūtra* it likewise says** that if **sons of the Conquerors** who have previously attained the wisdoms of hearing and contemplating **this sacred,** profound **teaching** of the Mahāyāna **should meditate upon** and cultivate the samādhi which is **without discrimination,** to the complete exclusion of conceptual fabrication of graspable characteristics, **they will** completely **escape the disturbances of** the net of **discrimination** of conceptual activities **and gradually achieve** completely **non-discriminating** primordial wisdom. As it says there,

> Should sons of the Conquerors contemplate
> This sacred teaching, without discrimination,
> They will escape the struggles of discrimination,
> And gradually achieve non-discrimination.

Therefore, non-discrimination is established scripturally in both sūtra and tantra.

*[End of the '1. Detailed explanation of how to train in higher insight']*

## 2. Concluding summary of how to train in higher insight

**58**
**With scriptures and reasoning,**
**Having made certain that all dharmas**
**Are nonarising, without intrinsic nature,**
**Meditate without discrimination.**

**With** the **scriptures** of definitive meaning **and** the flawless collections of **reasoning, having made certain** and cut any doubts **that** individuals and **all dharmas** such as the skandhas **are** in reality **nonarising,** or **without** arising with an **intrinsic nature, meditate** one-pointedly **without** the **discrimination** of grasping at characteristics in the natures of things. As it is said in Āryaśūra's *Jātakamāla,*

> Those who have heard this, take it to heart.
> You will be freed from the castle of birth
>   with little trouble.[20]

*[End of '1. Analytical presentation of the path (of the perfections)']*

## 2. Analytical presentation of the result

**59**
**Thus if one meditates upon suchness**
**And attains the successive stages of heat etc.,**
**Then one will attain the Joyful bhūmi and the rest,**
**And the enlightenment of a Buddha will not be far off.**

**Thus** on the basis of the common refuges, one trains one's mind on the paths of the lesser and intermediate persons, and then develops both aspiration and application bodhicitta. Together with the practices of vast skilful means, **one meditates upon suchness** with calm abiding and higher insight. If one does this, one will fully travel the lesser, intermediate and great stages of the path of accumulation, **and** then **attain the successive stages of heat etc.,** i.e. the four stages concordant to realisation comprising the path of application. **Then** one achieves **the** first **bhūmi,** called 'Joyful', the second bhūmi, called 'Immaculate', etc. until **one attains** the resultant conditions of the vajra-like samādhi at the tenth bhūmi. Then the result of the final completion of the path—**the** level of the great **enlightenment of a Buddha,** endowed with the three kāyas and five primordial wisdoms—**will not be far off** and will soon be attained. Activities of ripening and liberating limitless beings of good fortune will arise spontaneously and uninterruptedly for as long as saṃsāra exists. As it says in Maitreya's *Abhisamayālaṃkāra*,

> Accordingly, it is held that their activity
> Arises for as long as saṃsāra exists.

*[End of 'Detailed explanation of the characteristics of the superior person's path']*

## 2. Brief explanation of how to practise the mantra vehicle

1. Showing the necessity of entering into the Vajrayāna by attaining empowerment
2. Specific qualifications for those who would receive the two higher empowerments
3. Analysing whether it is appropriate to teach, hear etc. the tantras if the two higher empowerments have not been received

## 1. Showing the necessity of entering into the Vajrayāna by attaining empowerment

1. The individual who is the basis
2. The empowerment which ripens them
3. Showing the importance of the empowerment

## 1. The individual who is the basis

**60**
> With activities such as pacifying and increasing,
> And also with powers such as the eight great attainments,

> Like the excellent vase attainment,
> Which are accomplished through the power of mantra,

While one may come perfectly to fulfil the benefits of self and other by practising the six perfections and four gatherings in the tradition of the vehicle of the perfections, if one travels the path of the Vajrayāna **with** the four enlightened **activities, such as pacifying and increasing, and also with powers such as the eight great attainments, like the excellent vase attainment** which grants all of one's wishes,[21] then **accomplishment** will come **through the power of mantra**.

## 61

> If one wishes to fulfil completely with ease
> The accumulations of enlightenment,
> And if one wishes for the conduct of the secret mantras
> Taught in Kriyā, Caryā etc. tantras,

**If one wishes to** accomplish the **complete fulfilment** of **the accumulations of** great **enlightenment** for oneself and all benefits for others, **with ease** and swiftness, **and if one wishes** to practise properly all **the conduct of the secret mantras** according to how they are **taught in the** various divisions of the **tantras** such as the **Kriyā, Caryā etc.**, then one has the appropriate basis for the secret mantra Vajrayāna.

## 2. The empowerment which ripens them

**62**
**Then, for the ācārya empowerment,**
**One should please the holy lama with all one has,**
**Such as with veneration and with gifts, such as jewels,**
**And by accomplishing his instructions.**

**63**
**The one who pleases the lama**
**Will perfectly receive the ācārya empowerment.**

**Then,** once one has the basis of the Vajrayāna path, wishing to enter the secret mantra, one should please the holy lama who possesses the necessary qualities. Why should one do this? **For** the sake of receiving **the** vajr**ācārya empowerment**, as well as the three higher empowerments.[22] How should one do this? **One should please the holy lama** who bestows the empowerment **with all one has** of body, speech and mind, **such as with** physical and verbal **veneration, with gifts** of whatever goods he or she may wish for, **such as jewels**, garments, food and drink, and service, **and by accomplishing his instructions** perfectly and with dedication. As it says in Maitreya's *Mahāyānasūtrālaṃkāra*,

> One should rely on the spiritual friend by means of
> Respect, material goods, service and accomplishment.

**The one** disciple **who pleases the lama** in this way, having supplicated the lama for empowerment, **will** become a suitable vessel for the secret mantra by **perfectly receiving the** vajrācārya **empowerment** together with supporting permission initiations.

### 3. Showing the importance of the empowerment

> All of one's nonvirtues will be utterly purified
> And one will become worthy of
>   accomplishing siddhis.

For the **one** disciple who has perfectly received the four empowerments referred to above, **all of** their obscurations and **nonvirtues** of body, speech and mind, along with the imprints of these, **will be utterly purified and** that **one** disciple **will become worthy of accomplishing** all mundane and supreme **siddhis.**

*[End of '1. Showing the necessity of entering into the Vajrayāna by attaining empowerment']*

### 2. Specific qualifications for those who would receive the two higher empowerments

> **64**
> Because the great *Paramādibuddha* tantra
> Expressly forbids it,
> Those observing pure conduct
> Should not receive the secret and wisdom
>   empowerments.

Can anyone who wishes to attain siddhis receive these empowerments? **Because** the Bhagavān, in **the great** root **tantra** of the ***Paramādibuddha** Kālacakra,* made it **expressly forbidden**, laymen **observing pure conduct** and **those** monastics holding the discipline of the five kinds of monastic vows **should not receive** from others **the secret and wisdom empowerments,** nor bestow the empowerments themselves.

**65**
**Should these empowerments be received**
**By those keeping the discipline of pure conduct,**
**Because its conduct has been forbidden,**
**Their vows of discipline would be broken.**

What fault is there for those practising pure conduct etc. to take these two empowerments? **Should these** two **empowerments be** given, **received** etc. **by those keeping the discipline of pure conduct** or the monastic vows, **because its conduct has been forbidden** by the Buddha, **their discipline of** pure conduct or monastic **vows would be broken.**

**66**
**This would be a defeat**
**Of the discipline they were holding and a downfall,**
**And since they would be sure to fall into the lower realms,**
**They could not attain siddhis.**

**This would be defeat of the discipline** of moral conduct **they were holding and a** root **downfall**, which is similar to a defeat, **and since** someone who has committed a downfall **would be sure to fall into the** three **lower realms, they could not** thereafter **attain siddhis.** The Noble Lord said in his *Oral Instructions on the Middle Way called 'Opening the Jewel Casket'*,

> The secret and wisdom empowerments should not be given by those travelling the liberation path of pure conduct; nor should they be taken by disciples. Do not doubt that both the teacher and disciple who do so will extinguish their pure conduct and, since they are bringing about the decline of the teachings of the Buddha, be reborn in hell.

### 3. Analysing whether it is appropriate to teach, hear etc. the tantras if the two higher empowerments have not been received

**67**
**Hearing and explaining all the tantras,**
**Performing fire pūjās, offerings, and so forth,**
**Are not faults for those who have received**
**The ācārya empowerment and know**
  **thusness.**

If it is inappropriate for those who practise pure conduct to receive the two higher empowerments, are they also unable to practise the conduct of the secret mantras? There is no fault for them to do so.

For disciples to **hear all** of **the** four classes of tantra, such as Kriyā etc., **and** for teachers to **explain** them; for both to **perform fire pūjās,** make **offerings,** perform consecrations and so forth, **are not faults for those who have received** or obtained **the ācārya empowerment and know the** ten **thusnesses.**[23]

*[End of '2. Main exegesis of the text']*

### 3. The reason for composing the text

**68**
**Upon the supplication of Changchub-Ö,**
**I, the Sthavira Dīpaṃkaraśrī,**
**Have given this brief explanation of the path to enlightenment,**
**As I have seen it explained in teachings such as the sūtras.**

The divinely descended bhikṣu, **Changchub-Ö,** who propagated the Buddha's teachings in Tibet, **supplicated** thus: "You must certainly bestow upon us a text on the meaning of the whole of the Buddha's teaching which will be a chariot for Mahāyāna practitioners." **Upon** which, **the** Mahā**sthavira,** one who is a crown jewel of all of the eighteen Hīnayāna subsects, having received full ordination and held a perfectly unbroken continuity of vows for over thirty years, **Dīpaṃkaraśrī,** gave a complete **explanation of the** Mahāyāna **path** from the level of a beginner up **to** complete **enlightenment** in accord with what he **had seen explained in** precious **teachings such as the sūtras,** certain tantras, and explanatory śāstras.

As he said in his *Song of Developing A Resolute Mind Concerning Saṃsāra*,

> This life is short. Though we may know much,
> We do not know how much time we have.
> Like the swan separating milk from water,
> Separate your own wishes.

Thus, having discarded complicated conceptual systems of overstatement and diminishment, he **has given this brief explanation**, without verbosity, on the conditions for accomplishing the practices which lead to complete omniscience, without omitting anything.

*[End of '3. The text itself']*

## 4. Colophon

1. Who wrote the text
2. Who translated it

## 1. Who wrote the text

*The Lamp of the Path to Enlightenment*, **composed by the great ācārya Dīpaṃkara Śrījñāna is completed.**

This text which is called ***The Lamp of the Path to Enlightenment*, composed** for the benefit of countless fortunate disciples **by the great** learned **ācārya, Dīpaṃkara Śrījñāna,** the crown jewel of five hundred scholars, **is completed.**

## 2. Who translated it

**It was translated and checked by the great master of India himself and the great translator and editor, Gewa'i Lodro.**

**It was translated** from Sanskrit into Tibetan **and checked by the great master of India himself,** Dīpaṃkara Śrījñāna, **and the great translator,** the bhikṣu **Gewa'i Lodro** of Tibet, and having **edited** the words and meaning, they propagated this teaching.

> The one path travelled by all bodhisattvas,
> Who follow to thusness all the Conquerors of the ten directions,
> Is explained in this excellent text, now complete.
> May those wanting liberation obtain its innermost essence.
>
> In all births, under the care of spiritual friends,
> Having embarked upon this excellent path of truth and goodness,
> May supreme bodhicitta arise, stabilise and increase in them,
> And may they perfect an ocean of bodhisattva conduct.
>
> By the power of the compassion and aspiration prayers
> Of Śrī Dīpaṃkara, may we complete without difficulties

The graduated path to enlightenment,
And in this very life spontaneously
accomplish the two benefits.

Following the instruction of the Jetsun Lama, the great omniscient and compassionate one [Jamyang Khyentse Wangpo, 1820-1892], that it would be excellent if we were to render service to this great textual tradition, which is universally respected, in accord with the extant commentaries, Lodro Thaye, in emulation of a nonsectarian follower of the Buddha's teachings and holding merely the external signs of a bodhisattva, extracted the essence of the teachings of the sublime spiritual friends. May these writings cause virtue to increase.

# Notes

## Full Illumination of the Path to Enlightenment

1 Naktso Lotsāwa Tsultrim Gyalwa (*nag 'tsho lo tsa ba tshul khrims rgyal ba*) accompanied Atiśa to Tibet, studied under him for many years, and translated many texts in the Kangyur.

2 See Introduction for the three lineages of this teaching.

3 Dharmakīrti, learned in the system of Asaṅga, and the younger Vidyakokila (*rig pa'i khu byug chung ba*), also known as Avadhutipa, learned in the system of Nāgārjuna.

4 The *Blue Compendium* (*be'u bum sngon po*) contains teachings from the founding Kadampa masters Dromtonpa and Potowa, recorded by the latter's student Geshe Dolpa Sherab Gyatso (1059-1131). The full text has been translated by Ulrike Roesler in *The Stages of the Buddha's Teachings: Three Key Texts (10) (Library of Tibetan Classics)*, 2015, wherein this quotation is found

at pp. 58-59. David Jackson's introduction to that volume describes the *be'u bum* class of texts in some detail, as well as the *Blue Compendium* in particular, and other information on the nature of *lam rim*.

5   The remainder of this section is closely based on a passage in *The Graduated Path to Enlightenment, the Practices of the Three Persons (skyes bu gsum gyi nyams su blang ba'i byang chub lam rim pa)* by the Gelugpa patriarch Tsongkhapa Lozang Drakpa (*tsong kha pa blo bzang grags pa*, 1357-1419), an English translation of which has been published as *The Middle-Length Treatise on the Stages of the Path to Enlightenment* (Wisdom Publications, 2021. See chapter 7 for Tsongkhapa's version of the present passage).

6   The association of these three types of emptiness with the Hīnayāna reflects the influence upon the present passage of Tsongkhapa Lozang Drakpa (see Introduction and previous note), who held that the views of the Hīnayāna and Mahāyāna are the same, and that what differentiates the two vehicles is the duration upon which the view is meditated and the practice of the path. As he said:

> "Accordingly, the treatises of the noble master Nāgārjuna clearly state that even śrāvakas and pratyekabuddhas can know that all phenomena lack intrinsic existence. For, they state that liberation from cyclic existence is achieved through the view of emptiness of intrinsic existence. Śrāvakas and pratyekabuddhas meditate on that view for as long as their afflictions remain. When their afflictions

are extinguished, they are satisfied and do not persist in meditation; hence they are unable to eliminate cognitive obscurations. Bodhisattvas, not content with mere liberation from cyclic existence through the mere extinction of afflictions, seek buddhahood for the sake of all living beings; hence they meditate so as to utterly extinguish cognitive obscurations. Thus, they meditate for a very long time and are adorned with limitless collections of merit and wisdom." (*The Great Treatise on the Stages of the Path to Enlightenment, Volume 3*, Snow Lion 2014, p. 322-3).

Some masters, such as Goramapa Sonam Sengge, have criticized certain aspects of this position. While Gorampa agrees it is the opinion of both Nāgārjuna and Maitreya that śrāvakas and pratyekabuddhas do understand the emptiness of intrinsic existence, nevertheless it is not their primary doctrinal position and they do not take such emptiness as their principal mode of realization.

"As he says, [the śrāvaka path] does not take the lack of true existence of the skandhas as its main mode of realization. Instead, it takes the lack of true existence of the individual as its principal mode of realization. Likewise, the unobstructed path of seeing of the pratyekas can discard the apprehension of true existence which apprehends external phenomena as truly existent, because it takes the lack of true existence of external phenomena as its principal mode of realization." (*Distinguishing the Views: Moon Rays Illuminating the Crucial Points of the Excellent Vehicle*, Gorampa Sönam Senge, Vajra Books 2014, p. 119).

Therefore while the present passage in the commentary reflects the influence of Tsongkhapa, nevertheless, that it is the correct interpretation of Nāgārjuna and Maitreya is an opinion held in common with Gorampa. What Gorampa rejects is the further claim of Tsongkhapa that the Hīnayāna and Mahāyāna have the same view. For Gorampa, the Mahāyāna view is distinguished from that of the Hīnayāna by its teaching of freedom from the four kinds of proliferation, of which lack of true existence comprises only the first. This first mode of emptiness is, as already noted, a teaching also found in the Hīnayāna. Furthermore, it is only by freedom from the four kinds of proliferation that bodhisattvas are able to dispel cognitive obscurations, and not by meditating on the same view as Hīnayānists but for a longer time, as held by Tsongkhapa.

7  This section uses the scheme of the 'Four Branches of Purpose and Relation', *dgos 'brel yan lag bzhi*, Skt. anubandha-catuṣṭaya: an explanatory system from the Sanskrit literary tradition concerning the purpose of a textual composition. The four branches are (i) the *explanandum* (*brjod bya*) or subject to be explained, (ii) the immediate purpose (*dgos pa*) or reason for explaining, (iii) the meta-purpose (*dgos pa'i dgos pa*) or reason why the immediate purpose is sought and (iv) the relation (*'brel ba*), i.e. how the *explanans* (*rjod byed*) relates to or brings about the immediate purpose.

NOTES

8   The *rgyu 'bras man ngag bdun* (or *yan lag bdun*) is a system of instructions transmitted by Atiśa for developing bodhicitta by meditating in stages, of which the first six are the causes and the seventh is the result, i.e. bodhicitta itself.

9   In the *Sūtra Requested by Kāśyapa*, a sūtra belonging to the *Ratnakūṭa* collection, it says that in order to remember bodhicitta in future lives, one should abandon the four negative factors—(i) deceiving the lama or those worthy of offerings, (ii) causing someone to regret something which should not be regretted, (iii) disparaging a bodhisattva who is generating bodhicitta, and (iv) conducting oneself with pretense and deceit. It also says one should take up the four positive factors—(i) never lying, (ii) having altruism towards sentient beings without deceit, (iii) perceiving bodhisattvas as the Buddha and praising them, and (iv) encouraging others to enlightenment. See Sapan, *Clarifying the Sage's Intent*, trans. David Jackson (2015), pp. 412-413.

10  Sapan, *sdom gsum rab byed*, chapter 1, verses 204-5: 'Therefore, the sūtras and śāstras explain evil deeds with two classifications: inherent misdeeds and attendant misdeeds. Inherent misdeeds are misdeeds for all beings, while attendant misdeeds are subsequent downfalls attendant to vows.' See *A Clear Differentiation of the Three Codes*, trans. Rhoton, 2002, p.67.

11 *Rnal 'byor pa chen po dgon pa ba dbang phyug rgyal mtshan* (1016-1082): a disciple of Atiśa and abbott of *rwa sgreng* (Reting) monastery after the passing of Dromtonpa in 1064.

12 Most of this passage is absent from Kongtrul Rinpoche's commentary, but since verse 21 of the root text would lack any interlinear exegesis without it, I believe the omission must be a typographical error, and so I have restored it based on Panchen Lozang Chokyi Gyaltsen's commentary accordingly.

13 This quotation does not seem to belong to the *Samādhirāja Sūtra*. Panchen Lozang Chokyi Gyaltsen's commentary gives three quotations here, all attributed to the *Samādhirāja Sūtra*, of which this is the second and the only one that has made it into the extant edition of Kongtrul Rinpoche's commentary. However only the first belongs to the *Samādhirāja Sūtra*.

The first of Panchen Lozang Chokyi Gyaltsen's three quotations, and the only one sourced from the *Samādhirāja Sūtra*, is slightly mis-stated in his commentary as '*dge slong dngos po mchog tu bya ba yis*' instead of the '*dge slong dngos po mchog tu bya dka' yis*' found in the Degé Kangyur, Toh 127, vol. 55 (*mdo sde, Da*, folio 114a). In the latter version it seems these lines are spoken *to* the bhikṣu, saying that bodhicitta is 'supremely difficult to realise', rather than that the bhikṣu is 'the supreme mode' for bodhicitta, and extant English translations of this passage concur.

The second quotation is the one found in present editions of Kongtrul Rinpoche's commentary, and is attributed there to the *Samādhirāja Sūtra,* but the line in question is not found in that sūtra. It is found in Puṇḍarīkā's *Stainless Light* (Toh. 1347, vol. *Da,* f. 91a3-4), where it is attributed to the *Kālacakra* root tantra. In full the quotation is: 'Among the three, bhikṣu is supreme, intermediate / the sramanera is called, / and the upāsaka remains inferior' (*gsum las dge slong mchog yin 'bring, dge tshul zhes bya de dag las, khyim na gnas pa tha ma'o*), although only the first line is given in the present commentary, just as in Panchen Lozang Chokyi Gyaltsen. However, the quotation's intended topic is Vajrayāna and it concerns not the development of bodhicitta but the qualities of a Vajrācārya. For a translation of this quote in its proper context, see Kongtrul, Jamgon, *The Treasury of Knowledge: Book Five: Buddhist Ethics*, trans. Kalu Rinpoche Translation Group, Snow Lion 2003, p. 50 and p. 345, n. 55.

The third quotation of Panchen Lozang Chokyi Gyaltsen ('The receptacles of the precious flame of the Buddha's doctrine are the sons of Śākyamuni, the ascetics with saffron robes, the bhikṣus'), is in other texts attributed to another tantric source, the *Mañjuśrīmūlakalpa*, although I have not been able to locate it. One such attribution of it to the *Mañjuśrīmūlakalpa* is found in Jetsun Drakpa Gyaltsen's '*Dispelling Errors, An Illuminating Commentary on the Fourteen Root Downfalls*' (*rtsa ba'i ltung ba bcu bzhi pa'i 'grel pa gsal byed 'khrul spong, sa skya bka' 'bum,* Volume 7, pp. 275-410, translated by Lama Jampa Thaye, Ganesha Press 2003), wherein the author explains that the vows of bhikṣu, sramanera and upāsaka all lead to the higher realms, but only the first two lead to the state of an arhat. None of the prātimokṣa vows however lead directly to Buddhahood in the Mahāyāna. For the Mahāyāna bhikṣu, therefore, the possibility of prātimokṣa infractions is a great danger for a relatively small benefit, so it may seem to be a disadvantage for the Mahāyāna path. Nevertheless, being the 'root of the doctrine', the bhikṣu is training the mind in benefitting others, and thus is led towards the Mahāyāna (*theg chen por bkri ba*).

While we may not have determined the scriptural source for Atiśa's statement that the Brahmā conduct is supreme for developing bodhicitta, Atiśa's own personal authority should be sufficient for us to accept this point, especially since, according to Atiśa's biographies, he himself was encouraged by his teacher, Rahulaguptavajra, and inspired by prophetic visions, to take the Mahāsāṃghika ordination in order to benefit others, even after he had received and practiced many Mahāyāna and Vajrayāna teachings.

14 The verses numbered here 22 and 23 are in the reverse order in the root text. Panchen Lozang Chokyi Gyaltsen mentions that presenting them in this order is easier to explain ('*sngar blangs pa ni,'chad bde ba'i dbang du byas so*').

15 Panchen Lozang Chokyi Gyaltsen says of this text, '[Atiśa's auto] commentary [to the *Lamp of the Path to Enlightenment*] teaches the conditions of samādhi according to the *Tract on the Accumulation of Samādhi* composed by Ācārya Bodhibhadra.' He then mentions the seven conditions or factors [*yan lag*] of samādhi listed there and quotes Geshe Sharawa: '[The *Accumulation of Samādhi*] was translated by Lotsawa Gewa'i Lodro, who heard it from the Noble Lord himself. [Asaṅga's] *Srāvakabhūmi*, the introduction to [Atiśa's] *[Śrīguhyasamāja] Lokeśvara sādhana,* and Bodhibhadra's *Tract on the Accumulation of Samādhi* and so forth all teach [the conditions of samādhi].' There are some differences in the conditions listed in these three texts but no contradictions. Panchen Lozang Chokyi Gyaltsen adds that his own master held that the thirteen conditions listed in the *Srāvakabhūmi* were very important, and Zhangrompo even said all thirteen were essential, but the Panchen Lama himself mentions just four conditions: pure moral conduct, few desires, contentment, and staying in isolation.

16 This statement reflects the influence of Tsongkhapa on the commentary (see Introduction). He held that the views of the Hīnayāna and Mahāyāna are the same and it is only the path which differentiates the two vehicles. However, this opinion has been criticised by some masters, such as Goramapa Sonam Sengge: see note 6.

17 *'gang rnams rten cing 'brel bar byung [corrected from 'bad] / de rnams ngo bo nyid kyis med'* A gloss of the lines is found in the *Sāgaramati Sūtra* (H153: vol. 58, 73b.74a.1) *rten cing 'brel par gang byung ba / de dag gang la'ang rang bzhin med / gang dag ngo bo nyid med par/ de dag gang du'ang 'byung ba med:* 'What arises in dependence and connection / Is that which has no intrinsic nature / What has no essence / Is that which does not arise.'

18 The remainder of this section is closely based on a passage in Tsongkhapa's *skyes bu gsum gyi nyams su blang ba'i byang chub lam rim pa,* an English translation of which is published in chapter 24 of *The Middle-Length Treatise on the Stages of the Path to Enlightenment* (Wisdom Publications, 2021).

19 This quotation is found at H157, vol. 58, 349a.7, a versified form of a longer prose passage. The mastery of 'concern' [*bag yod*] by the bodhisattva who cognises emptiness is a recurring theme in this sūtra and is associated there with mindfulness and clear comprehension, as similarly elucidated in Śāntideva's *Bodhicaryāvatāra*.

20 *tshogs chung* corrected to *tshegs chung*. In some sources, *rdzong* (castle) is *rdzing* (lake).

21 There are different versions of the list of eight accomplishments but common inclusions are pills, clairvoyance, swift feet, eye-salve (for finding treasure), travelling underground, invisibility, flying, etc.

## NOTES

22 The vajrācārya empowerment is the culmination of the vase empowerment and is here a synonym for it. The vase empowerment is the principal empowerment of yoga tantra and the first of four levels of empowerment in the highest yoga tantra, i.e. vase, secret, wisdom and word empowerments.

23 The 'ten thusnesses' (Skt. *daśatattva*, Tib. *de kho na nyid bcu*) refers to specific qualifications for the bestowal of Vajrayāna empowerments (as in, for example, Ḍombipa's eponymous *Daśatattva*, which was known to Atiśa, who co-translated it into Tibetan). Atiśa's use of the term 'thusness' (*tattva*) here also indicates knowledge of the nature of dharmas. In Atiśa's auto-commentary, *Bodhimārgapradīpapañjikā*, he refers to the thusness of dharmas, or the nonarising of dharmas, and mentions several authoritative sources in this context.

Publishing finished
in September 2024 by Pulsio
Publisher Number: 4024
Legal Deposit: September 2024
Printed in Bulgaria